※ INSIGHT POCKET GUIDE

THAILAND

Discovery CHANNEL

APA PUBLICATIONS

Part of the Langenscheidt Publishing Group

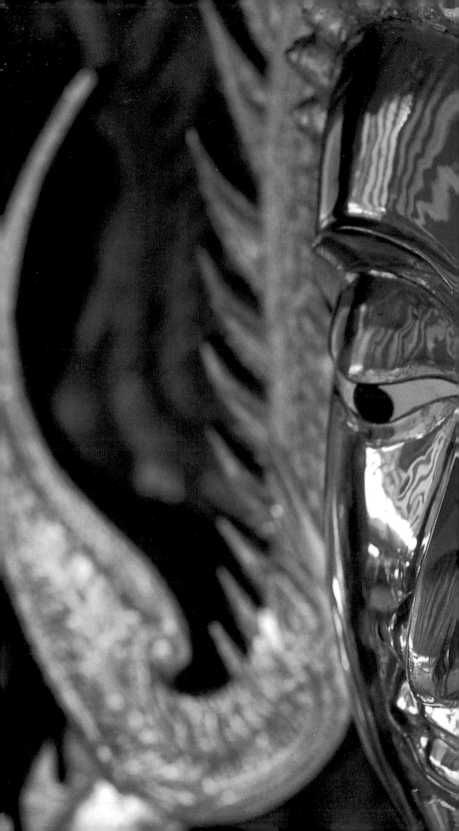

4

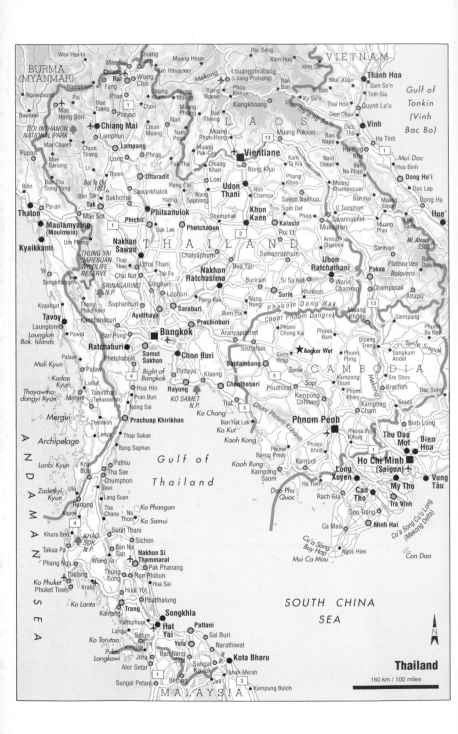

Welcome

This is one of 133 itinerary-based Pocket Guides produced by the editors of Insight Guides, whose books have set the standard for visual travel guides since 1970. With top-quality photography and authoritative recommendations, this guidebook brings you the very best of Thailand in a series of 22 itineraries devised by Insight's Thailand correspondent, Steve Van Beek.

For centuries, Thailand's magnetic appeal has turned many a short-term traveller into a frequent visitor. What is the lure behind this fabled kingdom? For one thing, it's Thailand's cultural diversity, with its multitude of ethnic influences and a rich art and architectural tradition spanning centuries. It is also a country in transition, filled with a dynamism that has transformed the landscape and made Thailand into what it is today. But most of all, it is the people: the Thais are a gentle race, gracious and tolerant of outsiders' foibles to a fault.

To help you uncover the secrets of Thailand, a series of carefully planned itineraries have been devised – using Bangkok, North Thailand, the Northeast and South Thailand as hubs. Designed to be flexible, the itineraries will help you get the most out of the country whether you're there for a few days or a few weeks. Pick from a selection of full- and half-day tours, and overnight excursions covering sights as diverse as boisterous street markets and fabled ancient cities to verdant jungles and sparkling turquoise seas. Chapters on shopping, eating out and nightlife, plus a useful practical information section on travel essentials complete this reader-friendly guide.

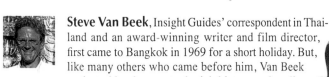

Steve Van Beek, Insight Guides' correspondent in Thailand and an award-winning writer and film director, first came to Bangkok in 1969 for a short holiday. But, like many others who came before him, Van Beek was so captivated by the country's rich history and traditions, and its charming people that he stayed on. When asked why he eventually made Bangkok his home, Van Beek says without hesitation, 'The more I discovered about the country, the more enthralled I became. I am hooked for life.'

6 contents

Pages 2/3: gilded Buddha images
Pages 8/9: a medley of Thai dishes

History
&Culture

Although bordering the ancient civilisations of China and India, Thailand is a relatively young country. Superbly crafted Bronze-Age implements and pottery found in the northeastern town of Ban Chiang suggest that a sophisticated culture flourished here, perhaps as early as 3,500 BC. Details of its history, however, are vague. From the 6th to the 8th century AD, Buddhist communities comprising Mon peoples from southern Burma were established west of present-day Bangkok at Nakhon Pathom, 180km (112 miles) north at Lopburi.

Beginning in the 11th century, the Khmers, who built the great city of Angkor, invaded from the east and established large cities at Lopburi and Sukhothai. In the 13th and 14th centuries, several Thai princes in the Mekong Valley united to defeat the Mon rulers in the north and the Khmer Empire of the central region. Many elements of Thai language, art and religion have clear Khmer origins. Till today, remains of Khmer monuments can be seen in Kanchanaburi and throughout the northeastern region of Thailand.

Birth of the Nation

Thailand's history as a nation began in the far north. Scholars are still debating whether proto-Thais drifted north through the mountains to settle in southern China, or arose in southern China and moved south into Thailand under the pressure of a growing population and the invading Mongol hordes of Genghis Khan. The latter is the more persuasive hypothesis. Thai communities and dialects still exist in southern China, Vietnam and Burma. The dominant groups in Laos – highland and lowland Lao – are also Thai who speak the same dialect as the people of northeastern Thailand.

By the 13th century, the Thais were well established in Chiang Saen on the Mekong River, and in Chiang Rai on the Kok River, a Mekong tributary. In the latter half of the 13th century, King Mengrai of Chiang Rai moved into the valley of the Ping River to establish a new capital at Chiang Mai in 1296.

Meanwhile, other Thai groups had filtered south through the mountains to the head of the Chao Phraya River valley. They took over the Khmer city of Sukhothai and in 1238, King Intradit formed a confederation of cities which eventually became the nation of Thailand, or Siam as it was then known.

Its greatest king, Ramkhamhaeng, was an ally of Mengrai, and with peace established between them, both kingdoms flourished in the fertile valleys. It was under Ramkamhaeng that a written language, derived from Sanskrit, was formulated and many of the monuments of Sukhothai were erected. The tradition of Buddhist scholarship established in Lopburi was also continued.

Left: ruins at Sukhothai
Right: terracotta image

The Kingdom of Ayutthaya

A preoccupation with religion at the expense of military affairs led to the downfall of Sukhothai. The threat came from a vassal state to the south, the ancient, Indianised settlement of Ayutthaya. Beginning in 1351, Ayutthaya launched military campaigns that within a few years claimed vassals throughout central Siam, lower Burma and the Malayan peninsula. By 1430, the kingdom had won military victories against Chiang Mai and Angkor.

The 400-year reign of Ayutthaya was frequently marred by wars with Burma. In 1569, the Burmese plundered Ayutthaya and moved much of the population to Burma. Twenty years earlier, Ayutthaya had fended off a Burmese invasion with the assistance of Portuguese mercenaries. The Portuguese had also taught the Siamese how to make cannons and muskets.

In the first half of the 16th century, Portuguese traders were the first Europeans to settle in Ayutthaya. As the city was a wealthy trading centre, communities of Dutch, French, British and Japanese soon followed. Japanese mercenaries also served as the king's guards. A small but influential number of Persian traders became intimate royal advisers and intermarried with the vast royal family; to this day, their descendants remain influential.

The most famous foreigner, however, was a Greek named Constantine Phaulkon, who became well-known in the court of King Narai. Formerly a cabin boy with the East India Company, he was a talented linguist and interpreter who rose to become the most trusted adviser of King Narai, who ruled from 1656 to 1688. Narai had become anxious about the economic designs of the Dutch and had welcomed the British traders as a counterweight. He looked most favourably on the French, possibly as a result of the influence of Phaulkon, who had by then converted to Catholicism.

The accounts of French Jesuit missionaries in Ayutthaya convinced King Louis XIV of France that a massive conversion of the Siamese 'heathen' might be possible. Two Siamese envoys visited the court of the Sun King and there were reciprocal visits of French envoys in 1685. During the latter visit, Phaulkon persuaded the French envoys that a small, well-equipped military force could quickly hasten the Christian conversion. The French ship arrived soon after.

Already suspicious of the Greek's extravagance and his relationship with the king, a faction in the Siamese court was now alarmed enough to confine the ailing king to his palace and to arrest Phaulkon. The latter was executed outside Lopburi on the site of his mansion while Narai died the following month. The succeeding kings in the next 150 years maintained a modest amount of foreign trade, but the open-door policy of Narai was abandoned.

While religious and earthly affairs flourished in Ayutthaya, the military power of the Third Burmese Empire was on the rise, and continued their attacks on Ayutthaya. Repelled in 1760, the Burmese plundered Ayutthaya after a 14-month siege in 1767. Many of the artefacts of four centuries of civilisation were burned to the ground. In the tradition of the times, most of the city's inhabitants and the royal family, totalling about 90,000 people, were taken back to Burma.

Bangkok's Rise

In 1782, the new king, Rama I, established Bangkok as his capital. He asked riverside Chinese merchants to move southeast to the Sampeng area which subsequently became the city's chief mercantile centre. On the land they vacated, he began construction of Wat Phra Kaeo – the Temple of the Emerald Buddha – to hold the kingdom's most famous Buddha image.

Prisoners of war were employed to dig defensive moats in concentric arcs to the east of Khlong Lord, the original canal (*khlong*). Rama I strove not only to establish a capital, but also to create a new Ayutthaya with symbols evoking its past grandeur and glory. The royal name for the city included the appellation Krung Thep, 'City of Angels', by which Ayutthaya had been known and the name modern Thais use for Bangkok.

Thailand again opened its doors to the outside world. By the 1830s, missionaries and a few merchants were living and working in the city and by 1860, trade and amity treaties had been established with the United States and many countries in Europe.

The two kings who are credited with modernising Thailand were King Mongkut (1851–68) and his son King Chulalongkorn (1868–1910). Mongkut, a remarkable man, built the city's first paved street, New Road, in 1863. King Chulalongkorn continued the modernisation process, building a railway line north, adding more city roads, constructing a tram line, and erecting western-style public buildings.

As Bangkok moved into the 20th century, it grew eastwards and northwards. Silom Road changed from a rural area of cattle markets, rice fields and market gardens into a residential neighbourhood. In 1932, the

Left: Burmese ship in a battle against Thais
Above: Phaulkon's palace at Lopburi. **Right:** King Rama I

Memorial Bridge, the city's first, was built to link Bangkok and Thonburi and this spurred development on the western side of the river.

The city's big construction boom came in the 1960s during the Vietnam War when vast amounts of money poured into Thailand. The two-lane road that led to Don Muang Airport was widened to four lanes and then, in the 1970s, to 10 lanes. The 1980s saw the city alter direction from horizontal to vertical, with the skyline changing almost weekly. The economic boom of the late 1980s and early 1990s changed the city forever and its population has burgeoned to well over 10 million people.

Lanna: A Separate Identity

Lanna, 'Land of a Million Rice Fields', is the name by which the north of Thailand is known. Until the early part of the 20th century, it existed as a separate kingdom with its own royal house, dialect and culture. The north's history begins with King Mengrai who marched south from Chiang Saen to establish the city of Chiang Rai in 1262. After capturing Haripunchai (Lamphun) and securing joint leadership of Phayao, he sought a more central site in the Ping River Valley and established Chiang Mai (New City) in 1296.

The flowering of Lanna culture dates from the reign of warrior King Tilokaraja. He was so influential that the Eighth World Buddhist Council was held in Chiang Mai in 1455. A century later, an earthquake destroyed parts of the city, including a portion of the great stupa of Wat Chedi Luang.

Chiang Mai fell to the Burmese king of Pegu in 1558 and was ruled by Burma for the next two centuries. The hardships became so severe that, as in several other cities of the north, the inhabitants abandoned it for 20 years until Prince Kawila re-populated it in 1796, and then triumphed over the Burmese in 1799.

A railway, begun in 1898 and completed in 1921, enabled the north to develop links with Bangkok. In 1939, Chiang Mai was upgraded to a province and brought under the aegis of the Bangkok administration.

The Distant South

The history of Southern peninsular Thailand is lesser known than that of the north. It was once under the control of the mighty Srivijaya Empire, which existed from the 7th to the 13th century. Certainly Chaiya, near present day Surat Thani, was an important city within that empire. The Srivijaya Empire disintegrated during the 13th century and its dependencies were absorbed by the burgeoning Sukhothai Empire.

Above: Prince Kawila, hero of Chiang Mai

History first takes note of Phuket in the *Kedah Annals* from Malaysia, which were written around 1200. The island was shared from an early date by Mon people from Burma who occupied the northern region and the Chao Ley (sea gypsies) who settled along the southern coast. Phuket had a reputation among 17th-century European sea captains for harbouring pirates, but by the 18th century, European ships were calling to load up with water, firewood and pitch to caulk their boats. Later, merchants traded European products for local ivory, gems and pearls.

When tin was discovered on the island in the 1840s, Phuket Town became the most important settlement in southern Thailand and within a few decades it dominated the island's economic life. By the 1900s, rubber plantations blanketed the hills, not only of the island but also much of the south. Today, tourism is the region's main money-earner, and Phuket, Krabi and Ko Samui are major holiday destinations for both Asian and Western tourists.

The People

Whether the original inhabitants were indigenous peoples or migrants from China or Burma, their ethnic blood has been augmented by Vietnamese, Cambodian, Lao, Mon, Malay, Indian and even Persian strains to create a race recognisable as Thai. The most prominent minority is the Chinese who, while retaining much of the culture of the Middle Kingdom, have been absorbed into the Thai fabric, making Thailand rare among Asian countries in having avoided class, ethnic and religious wars.

Northern and northeastern culture betray Lao strains while the south has been richly endowed by its proximity to the Muslim culture of Malaysia. For most visitors, the animistic hill tribes are the north's most colourful inhabitants. Each of the six principal groups – Hmong (Meo), Lisu, Akha, Lahu (Musur), Mien (Yao) and Karen – has a distinct language incomprehensible to the others. With ancient origins in China, they arrived in northern Thailand in the 19th century.

Except for the Karen, most hill tribes have traditionally practised slash-and-burn farming; when the soil was exhausted, a village would move to a new site. Today, there is no place left to move. In the past two decades, international and Thai projects have encouraged the hill tribes to grow cash crops and phase out opium cultivation. Success has been mixed. Due to illiteracy, land shortages, lack of land rights and citizenship, tribal cultures are in danger of extinction.

A quarter of Phuket's official population of 270,000 live in Phuket Town. Most are Thais who have migrated from the mainland, along with Chinese who arrived to work the tin mines in the mid-1800s and Muslims of Malay extraction. The most interesting of the original inhabitants are the Chao Ley, a nomadic people who travelled from island to island in search of food. Reputed to have originated from the Andaman and Nicobar islands between Burma and India, they are dark skinned and have dark, curly hair. They speak Yawi, which is quite similar to the language used by the indigenous Malays of neighbouring Malaysia.

Right: a Northern Thai

Thai Culture

Everything that one associates with the exotic Orient – fabulous palaces, glittering temples, beautiful Buddha images, ornate art – is found in abundance in Thailand. The Thais have a delicate touch which transforms ordinary objects into works of art, a skill they have applied to a wide range of practical objects and art works.

Although having many antecedents, Thai art has a unique style. The country has also produced a variety of applied arts, most of them for the purpose of beautifying temples: mother-of-pearl decorates temple doors and royal utensils; scenes in black and gold lacquer often cover temple doors and windows; murals on the inner walls of the temples tell the story of Buddha's life or of his last incarnations before being born as the Buddha.

Dance and drama have been the principal mode of transmitting ancient stories, with the *Ramakien* being the most important source for theatrical productions. This is the Thai version of the Indian classical tale, the *Ramayana*, which tells the story of the abduction of the beautiful Sita, wife of the god-king Phra Ram, by the treacherous demon king Tosakan.

Chiang Mai is considered the cultural capital of Thailand, and its temples are among the most beautiful in Asia. While the Lanna or northern style has been heavily influenced by Burmese architectural styles, its architects and artists have evolved a distinct style that differs from the dominant 'central Thai' style.

The southerners were not monument builders, so there is little architecture of consequence. It is in the realm of theatre that they excelled. During a stay in Phuket, you may view one of the two most famous southern creations, the *Manohra* (a dance-drama telling the story of a bird-goddess who falls in love with a human) and the *Nang Talung* (shadow puppet theatre).

Thai Values

The oft-repeated phrase '*mai pen rai*' expresses a common Thai attitude. It translates as 'it doesn't matter', 'never mind' or 'no problem'. Foreign visitors often hear it when they discover they've committed a *faux pas*. Thais will play down such errors in pursuit of smooth social relations.

Compared to many other Asian women, Thai women historically have had considerable freedom of movement. Unfortunately, as the prevalence of prostitution attests, girls from poor Thai families have less education, fewer opportunities and weaker legal rights than their brothers. In the sphere of the wealthy elite, however, many women occupy powerful positions. Some major companies are helmed by formidable Thai women, and women are also prominent in academia and the professions.

Above: detail from a Thai *sala*, or pavilion

HISTORY HIGHLIGHTS

3,500 BC: Bronze Age culture thrives at Ban Chieng in northeast Thailand.

8th–12th century: Thais migrate from China into northern Thailand.

1238: King Intradit establishes an independent nation based in Sukhothai.

1350: Ayutthaya supplants Sukhothai as Thailand's capital.

1767: Burmese armies destroy Ayutthaya. Thai army regroups at Thonburi and engages in 15 years of wars with the Burmese, Lao and Vietnamese.

1782: Wars end. General Chakri (Rama I) assumes the throne, establishing the Chakri dynasty. He moves his headquarters across the river to Bangkok.

1851–68: King Mongkut (Rama IV) ascends the throne, reforms the laws and sets Thailand on the path towards modernisation.

1868–1910: King Chulalongkorn (Rama V) continues his father's initiatives. He preserves the sovereignty of Thailand, the only Southeast Asian nation that escapes colonisation.

1910–25: King Vajiravudh (Rama VI) concentrates on modernising the country. Thailand sides with the Allies during World War I.

1925–35: Economic troubles compound King Prajadhipok's (Rama VII) problems. In 1932, a coup takes place and Prajadhipok is forced to accept a provisional constitution that makes him a figurehead. He abdicates in 1935.

1935–46: Ananda Mahidol (Rama VIII) is named king but remains in Switzerland to complete his studies. The Japanese occupy Thailand during World War II. In 1946, King Ananda dies and is succeeded by his younger brother, Bhumibol Adulyadej.

1950–72: On 5 May, Prince Bhumibol is crowned King (Rama IX). The 1950s is a time of turmoil, with a succession of military-backed governments. In the 1960s, Thailand enjoys an economic boom due to investment by the US.

1973–91: On October 1973, bloody clashes between the army and students bring down the military government, but political and economic blunders cause the new civilian government to fall just three years later. Various military-backed and civilian governments come and go for almost 20 years.

1992: Another violent clash between the army and students ending with the reinstatement of a new civilian goverment under Chuan Leekpai.

1995–97: In July, the Chart Thai party is elected. Two weak, corrupt governments mismanage the economy. The Thai baht is devalued in July 1997 and Thailand enters a recession.

1998: A new Democrat government led by the former prime minister Chuan Leekpai takes over.

2000–01: Economy improves. Thaksin Shinawatra, the leader of the Thai Rak Thai (TRT) party, comes into power in the January 2001 elections.

2004: A tsunami generated by a 9.0-Richter earthquake in the Indian Ocean wrecks great loss of life and property along Thailand's Andaman coastline.

2005: Thaksin Shinawatra and his TRT party wins a landslide victory in the general elections.

2006: Thaksin is accused of evading taxes after selling his family-owned company. Mass protests take place in Bangkok and Thaksin is deposed by a military coup while he is overseas.

2007: Surayud Chulanont is appointed as interim prime minister while a new constitution is drafted. In the December elections, a Thaksin-endorsed party called the PPP triumphs. Samak Sundaravej is appointed as prime minister.

2008: Thaksin returns to Thailand and faces trial for corruption.

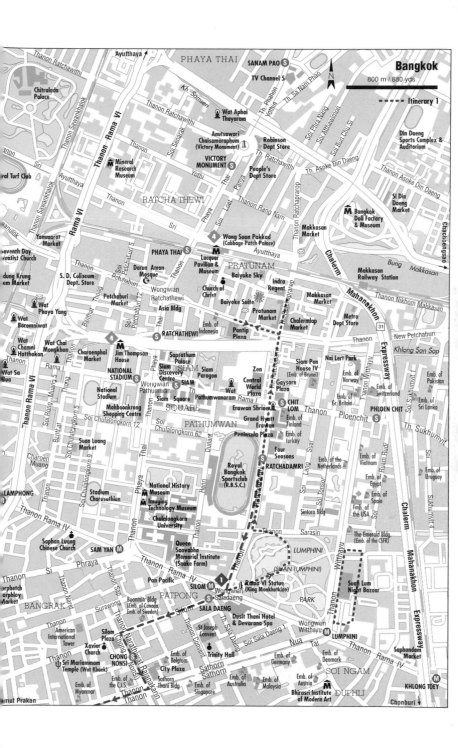

Bangkok

800 m / 880 yds

- - - - Itinerary 1

Bangkok & Environs

B angkok is Thailand's capital city, whose dominance over the rest of the country is so absolute that it has the ability to shape the nation's perceptions and directions. With an estimated 10 million people, many of whom are migrants, its only distant rival in terms of population size is the northern city of Chiang Mai, which hosts 1.5 million people.

Bangkok's haphazard growth over the past few centuries presents a challenge for visitors finding their way around. Lacking a grid system, Bangkok's streets can have as many as four different names along their lengths. There is no distinct business district, nor are there any easily identifiable landmarks. Many shops, restaurants and houses don't display street numbers. While the heat, humidity and traffic congestion all conspire against making this a city for walkers, the sights and sounds of one of Asia's most exuberant and culturally rich cities will amply reward those who persevere. There are lanes and alleys to wander where you'll discover many of Bangkok's secrets and although few Thais are fluent in English, they are ever willing to help. Stop a Thai to ask directions and, likely as not, he or she will personally walk you to your destination. Crime against tourists is fairly rare, but as in all big cities, it pays to be on your guard.

Full-day itineraries 1 and 2 offer a flavour of the city, while half-day itineraries 3 and 4 take you deeper into the city's heart. Although some of the tours involve a fair bit of walking, you can easily hop into a water taxi to escape the heat and traffic jams. With the introduction of two fully air-conditioned mass transit systems, the Skytrain (or BTS) and the MRT (also known as the metro or subway), travel within the city has become much more convenient, quicker, and more comfortable.

Bangkok's air-conditioned taxis are also one of the city's great bargains, but if you do take a taxi, try to avoid rush hour: 8–10am, 2–3pm (during school terms), 6–7pm and especially on Fridays. If caught in the thick of it, follow the Thai example: sit back and relax. Arm yourself with bottled drinking water – and, during the June to October rainy season, an umbrella.

Itineraries 5 to 12 are either long day trips or overnight excursions that take you beyond the city's limits, including a visit to a floating market, a boat trip to the ancient capitals of Ayutthaya, a rail trip to the infamous 'River Kwai Bridge', and sojourns in Hua Hin and Pattaya, both by the beach but utterly different from one another.

Admission to temples is free, or costs relatively little, and unless otherwise stated, are open daily from 8am–6pm, with last admissions at 5pm. Do dress respectfully and be prepared to remove footwear before entering the inner sanctuaries. Photography of most sites is permitted, excluding the Emerald Buddha in Bangkok.

Left: Buddha image at Wat Pho
Right: *tuk-tuk* are ubiquitous in Bangkok

1. BANGKOK'S HIGHLIGHTS *(see map, p18–19)*

An early morning stroll in Lumphini Park, followed by breakfast and a visit to the Erawan Shrine. Take the Skytrain to Central Pier for a cruise on the Chao Phraya River. A riverside lunch follows a visit to the National Museum of Royal Barges. Relax over an afternoon tea, or shop for souvenirs, and end the evening at the night bazaar and a puppet show.

Take a taxi to Lumphini Park, at the junction of Ratchadamri and Rama IV roads: entrance gates on all sides. Start at 7am to avoid the heat, or begin at the Erawan Shrine around 9am. The Chao Phraya Tourist Boat (see page 93) operates from 9.30am daily if you want to start with the cruise.

Lumphini Park (daily 5am–9pm; free) was named after the town in Nepal where the Buddha was born. The park wears many faces: in the morning,

the Chinese predominate; in the evening, the Thais; at night, it becomes the domain of some dubious low life and should be avoided. It's perfectly safe, though, to attend Thai kick-boxing matches which take place several evenings a week at the nearby Lumphini Boxing Stadium *(see page 84)*.

As the sun rises, joggers pound the park's pavements and office workers hurry to work, grabbing bowls of noodles from pavement vendors. Health-conscious Chinese perform *tai chi* exercises and would-be Chinese warriors mime ancient rituals with silver swords. Others prefer to take part in *en masse* aerobic displays performed to thumping disco music. By evening, joggers and keep-fit enthusiasts from nearby office towers flock to the park to enjoy a run around the lakes in the cooler hours.

Leave by the north gate to Sarasin Road, turn left and walk a short distance before turning right into Ratchadamri Road. Walk (or take a taxi if it's too hot) down this road and you will see the **Ratchadamri BTS Station** overhead. Further down this road you will pass the **The Four Seasons** and **Grand Hyatt Erawan** hotels. It's worth going inside the Four Seasons hotel to see the intricate foyer wall and ceiling murals, painted by one of the few remaining Thai artists specialising in this traditional style.

Erawan Shrine

The glittering **Erawan Shrine** (daily 24 hours) straddles the corner of Ratchadamri and Ploenchit roads, just opposite **Gaysorn** mall, an easy landmark to spot. You can join the Thai supplicants and buy incense, candles and flowers as offerings to the four-faced Hindu god Brahma. Though many Thais don't know it, this shrine is of Hindu

Above: Lumphini Park at dawn
Right: offerings at Erawan Shrine

origin, not Buddhist. Thais believe they can win at love or the lottery with their offerings. Throughout the day and night, ornately-garbed classical dancers perform to the accompaniment of traditional musicians. Beware of illegal touts demanding high fees for photographs.

Shopping Malls and Markets

If it's after 10am, check out the brand name boutiques that make up the luxury **Gaysorn** mall (tel: 0-2656 1177; daily 10am–8pm), or seek out the excellent contemporary homeware store **Cocoon** on its third floor. The huge **Central World** shopping centre (tel: 0-2635 1111) with its **Zen** department store (daily 10am–8pm) is diagonally opposite. The mall has many fast food outlets; access is via a pedestrian bridge from the Gaysorn.

Go past the two malls, and turn left onto busy Petchaburi Road, walk another 150m (450ft) to reach **Pantip Plaza** (daily 10.30am–8pm) an emporium selling hundreds of electronic gadgets and hi-tech accessories, as well as software. Just behind the Erawan Shrine, on the Ploenchit Road side, is **Sogo** (daily 10am–8pm), another huge department store.

To see a busy local street market, cross from the shrine to the Central World Plaza and continue to a busy bridge over a canal; this is **Khlong San Sap**, the north side serves as a landing for water taxis. It's possible to take a westbound boat all the way to Wat Saket and the Golden Mount, stopping off at Jim Thompson House *(see page 32)* along the way. The east-bound boats run parallel to New Petchaburi Road and up near Ramkhamhaeng University.

If you bypass the boats and continue up to Petchaburi Road, as Ratchadamri changes its name to Ratchaprarop, you will reach a busy junction. Crossing to the northeast corner, you arrive at one half of the vast **Pratunam Market** (daily 9am–6pm). Past the street vendors, look for a lane running to the right between buildings. Follow it and you will find yourself in a 'wet market' of fresh produce and kitchen items. Across the street is the other half of Pratunam, which sells cheap clothing.

If the clogged alleys and heat of this market becomes unbearable, retrace your steps back 1km (½ mile) to Ratchadamri BTS Station, and take a ride in air-conditioned luxury just four stops to the terminus, **Saphan Thaksin BTS Station.** In future this route will be extended across the river.

Take the BTS exit marked 'hotel shuttle boats' and go down the steps

to the **Central Pier** (also known as **Tha Sathorn Pier**). Here you can purchase all day, 'hop on, hop off' boat tickets (100 baht) valid for the **Chao Phraya Tourist Boat** (daily 9.30am–3pm; after 3pm, this ticket is valid on the regular express boats; www.chaophrayaboat.co.th). Next to the BTS, boats are probably the best way to get around in traffic-congested Bangkok.

Right: vendors at Pratunam Market

A Leisurely Cruise and Riverside Lunch

Sit back and enjoy the scenery as the boat slowly meanders past luxury hotels, more humble stilt homes and glittering Thai temples. On the left bank is the district of **Thonburi**; this particular stretch of the Chao Phraya displays the city's immensely cosmopolitan history. Among the tall palms and overgrown gardens, you may catch a glimpse of numerous delightful – if dilapidated – colonial mansions. These were once the homes of wealthy Sino-Portuguese traders; today some of them have been converted into shops and businesses.

Also on the left, the ochre-tiled **Kiang An Keng Pagoda** and its beautiful temple recall the importance of the city's early Chinese merchants and traders. On the same bank just a little further upstream is a green-domed mosque and then, a bit further on, the stately cream and red dome of the **Santa Cruz Church**, built by Portuguese missionaries.

As the boat cruises up the river it stops en route at both public and private piers. It continues under Memorial Bridge, stopping at **Tha Tien Pier** from where regular shuttle boats cross to **Wat Arun** (tel: 0-2891 1149; daily 8.30am–5pm; admission fee), or Temple of Dawn, whose giant tiled spire, called a *prang* in Thai, is visible from many miles away. After passing **Tha Chang Pier**, the stop for the Grand Palace and Wat Phra Kaew *(see page 26)*, the boat continues northwards passing under Phra Pin Klao Bridge before making a 'U' turn at **Banglamphu Pier**.

Make sure you get off at the next stop for the **National Museum of Royal Barges** (tel: 0-2424 0004; daily 9am–5pm; admission fee) by pressing the bell near the exit to alert the boat pilot. (In the low season, the boat sometimes drops off passengers on the right bank to connect with the cross-river ferry to the museum; just let the ticket collector know when you get on the boat.)

Kept here are the most important barges in the Royal Fleet of 51, which undertake grand river processions on special occasions; the last occurred in 2006 on King Bhumibol's 60th anniversary on the throne. The 44-m (144-ft) long vessel with the graceful swan-head prow is called the **Suphannahongse**, in which only members of the royal family are allowed to ride.

Catch the same boat back downstream and disembark two stops later at **Tha Maharaj Pier** from where a free ferry will take you to **Supatra River**

bangkok & environs

House (daily 11.30am–11.30pm; tel 02-411 0305), an award-winning Thai restaurant and theatre owned by a well-known patron of the arts. The serene courtyard restaurant offers indoor and outdoor dining overlooking the river and Wat Arun; on Friday and Saturday evenings it stages traditional Thai dance shows.

High Tea at the Oriental

After lunch, return to Maharaj Pier to catch the same boat service downstream. If you feel like a walk, get off at **Tha Tien Pier**, from where **Wat Pho** *(see page 28)* is a short 3-minute walk away. From the pier, take a first right at the main road – the temple's blue-tiled roof will be just opposite. Otherwise, continue on the cruise to the **Si Phraya Pier** next to **River City Shopping Complex** (tel: 0-2237 0077; daily 9am–8pm), a small shopping centre filled with handicraft and antiques shops.

If you are dressed smartly (no shorts or flip flops), indulge in afternoon tea in one of the luxury hotels along the river. A popular choice is the lovely **Author's Lounge** (daily 11am–8pm) at **The Oriental Hotel** (tel: 0-2659 9000; www.mandarin-oriental.com/bangkok). Ask for the boat to stop at Tha Oriental Pier. Established in 1876, The Oriental is where in times past luminaries such as Somerset Maugham, Noel Coward and Graham Greene have stayed. Order tea or freshly brewed coffee at the Author's Lounge and relax for a while under shady bamboo trees.

By now it will be early evening, so take the Skytrain back to your hotel if traffic is building up, or try to find the closest station, then hop in a taxi or *tuk-tuk* from there. If you want to linger at The Oriental for dinner, the hotel's **Sala Rim Naam Restaurant** (tel: 0-2437 6211) serves exquisite Thai food.

After dinner, visit the **Suan Lum Night Bazaar** (daily 3pm–midnight) at the corner of Rama IV and Witthayu roads, where you will find a huge array of bargain souvenirs, handicrafts and clothing. This is a good substitute if you don't have time to visit the Chatuchak Weekend Market. If you haven't had dinner, the Suan Lum bazaar has an array of restaurants and food stalls to try.

The **Joe Louis Theater** (tel: 0-2252 9683; www.joelouis-theater.com) performs a highly entertaining puppet show at 7.30pm nightly (admission fee) at the Suan Lum Bazaar. Using intricately made Thai puppets, stories from Thai folklore, including the Hindu epic *Ramayana*, are enacted.

Left: the haunting Wat Arun (Temple of the Dawn)
Above: royal barges
Right: tea at the Author's Lounge

2. WAT PHRA KAEW, GRAND PALACE AND WAT PHO
(see map below)

Breakfast at your hotel, then a walking tour to see Wat Phra Kaew and the Grand Palace complex. Next, the Coins and Decorations Museum followed by a visit to Wat Pho. Sample a Royal Thai, or alternatively, modern Thai-fusion dinner, in delightful surrounds.

Start your journey at Central (or Tha Sathorn) Pier (see page 23), or any public pier on the east bank where express boats leave regularly upstream.

Fares are only a few baht so have some small coins at hand. The slower Chao Phraya Tourist Boat leaves every half hour from Central Pier; if you catch it at any other pier, buy tickets on board for your stop at Tha Chang, or pay 100 baht for a day ticket that allows you to hop on and off anywhere you please.

When you get off the boat at **Tha Chang Pier**, the ornate **Grand Palace** roofs will be visible on your right. Walk about 200m (650ft) down the street to the entrance of the **Wat Phra Kaew** and **Grand Palace** complex (tel: 0-2623 5500; daily 8.30am–3.30pm; admission fee). No other temple complex so typifies Thai art as the Wat Phra Kaew, also known as the **Temple of the Emerald Buddha**. Its glittering surfaces and wealth of art makes it one of Asia's architectural wonders. The admission ticket also covers the Grand Palace, the Wat Phra Kaew Museum, the Coins and Decorations Museum and Vimanmek Mansion across town (see *Itinerary 3*).

Wat Phra Kaew was the first major architectural complex to be built in Bangkok. As you enter the complex, you will encounter an imposing trio of structures on your left. The first of these is the huge **Phra Si Rattana Chedi**, which is covered in gold mosaic tiles and said to enshrine a piece of the Buddha's breastbone. In the centre is the **Phra Mondop** (Library of Buddhist Scriptures), where the *Tripitaka*, or holy Buddhist scriptures, are stored. Adjacent to the Phra Mondop, the **Prasat Phra Thep Bidom** (Royal Pantheon) holds the statues of the first eight Chakri kings. Behind the Phra Mondop is a large detailed sandstone model of **Angkor Wat**. Along the northern edge of the model, you will also find **Viharn Yot** (Prayer Hall),

Above: Wat Phra Kaew
Right: Chakri Maha Prasat

flanked by **Ho Phra Nak** (Royal Mausoleum) on the left, and **Ho Phra Montien Tham** (Auxillary Library) on the right. Beginning opposite Viharn Yot, the 178 murals painted on the walls surrounding the temple complex recount the *Ramakien* epic.

Finally, you will come to the principal building of the Wat Phra Kaew complex, the *bot*, specially constructed to house the kingdom's most sacred **Emerald Buddha** image. Sitting high on a pedestal, the 66-cm (26-in) high jadeite image is surprisingly small. The fact that it is venerated in such a lavish manner, however, leaves no doubt about its importance to the Thais.

The Grand Palace

From Wat Phra Kaew, turn left into the compound where the **Grand Palace** is located. Since 1946, the Thai royal family has lived in Chitralada Palace in the Dusit area of Bangkok, but the Grand Palace is still used for state ceremonies and for receiving foreign dignitaries.

The first building of note on the left is the **Amarin Vinitchai Throne Hall** which served as a royal residence for Rama I, II and III, the first three kings of the Chakri dynasty. In the first hall is the boat-shaped throne where legal cases requiring royal adjudication were heard. Behind it was Rama I's bedchamber. Since his reign, each new monarch has slept there the first night after his coronation. In the courtyard are gold-knobbed red poles where the royal elephants were once tethered.

The next centrepiece is the majestic **Chakri Maha Prasat** (Grand Palace Hall) with its three spires atop an Italianate Renaissance building. Constructed in 1882, it was the last building to be erected in the Grand Palace. Wander through the state drawing rooms which are decorated in the manner of European palaces, with some Thai touches.

Further on the left is the **Dusit Maha Prasat** (Dusit Hall), where kings conducted state business. It is now the final resting place for deceased kings before they are cremated in the nearby Sanam Luang field. On the left of the complex is a lovely little restaurant with an open verandah, from where you get a panoramic view of the Dusit Maha Prasat. Just opposite is the **Wat Phra Kaew Museum**, which contains a collection of exquisite Bud-

dha images made of crystal, silver, ivory and gold as well as some beautiful lacquer screens. In the southern room on the second floor are two very interesting scale models of the Grand Palace/Wat Phra Kaew complex; one as it looked over 100 years ago and the other as it looks today.

On exiting the Grand Palace complex, turn right and walk past the ticket booth to the **Coins and Decorations Museum**. Here you will find a variety of ceramic coins, silver bullet money, seals and money from the other regions of Thailand and the world. Upstairs are royal crowns, jewelled swords, jewellery, brocaded robes and intricate betel nut sets.

Eclectic Wat Pho

Leave the complex north at Na Prathat Road and walk to your left along the wall in the direction of the river. At the corner, turn left again and walk along the Grand Palace wall. Pass the next junction and turn left at the second corner. A short way down on the left is the entrance to **Wat Pho** (tel: 0-2222 0933; daily 8am–6pm; admission fee), Bangkok's largest and oldest temple.

Restored many times, Wat Pho is one of the city's most eclectic temples. Of special interest is the 46-m (150-ft)-long gilded **reclining Buddha** in the northwest corner. Examine the soles of the feet which bear, in intricate mother-of-pearl patterns, the 108 signs by which a Buddha can be recognised. In the courtyard are statues of *rishi* (ascetics) demonstrating exercises to keep the body strong and limber. The tall stone temple guards in top hats were built to mimic early Dutch traders. Do not miss the *bot* (ordination hall) to the right of the entrance with its marvellous mother-of-pearl doors and its sandstone bas-relief panels depicting scenes from the classical *Ramakien* saga. Pull the stone ball from the mouth of a Chinese stone lion without breaking the ball or the mouth and you are said to be guaranteed eternal life.

On the eastern side of the courtyard is the **Wat Pho Thai Traditional Medical and Massage School** (daily 8am–6pm; tel: 0-2221 2974; www.wat pomassage.com), which offers good traditional massages for a small fee.

When you're done, head for **Poh Restaurant** (daily 6–10pm) at the nearby Tha Tien Pier. The lovely pierside setting compensates for the ordinary menu, which includes squid, mussels and shrimp with rice or noodles, a few curries, and numerous fish dishes. Sit upstairs for the best view across the river to Wat Arun. The restaurant stays open well after the kitchen closes.

3. WAT BENJAMABOPHIT AND VIMANMEK MANSION
(see map below)

See the Marble Temple at dawn and watch monks receive alms. Continue to the exquisite Vimanmek Mansion, former rustic royal home. This is the world's largest structure built entirely of teak; it houses a collection of art treasures and personal effects of the king.

About 6.30am ask a taxi driver to take you to Wat Benjamabophit at the junction of Rama V and Si Ayutthaya roads. Alternatively, bus numbers 2 and 72 stop nearby. The rest of the itinerary is best completed on foot.

Each morning before dawn, some 100,000 Buddhist monks throughout the kingdom don their saffron robes and walk barefoot through the streets. Buddhist families waiting outside their homes place rice and curries in the silent monks' black *baht* (alms bowls) which they will later eat at their monasteries. At **Wat Benjamabophit** (Marble Temple; tel: 0-2282 7413; daily 8am–5.30pm; admission fee) the ritual is slightly altered. At dawn, Thais take the food to the monks who wait in the tree-shaded street before the temple.

The almsgiving continues until 7.30am. Take all the photos you like and then enter the temple courtyard. Wat Benjamabophit was built in 1900, the last major temple built in Bangkok. Designed in cruciform shape, the *viharn* (prayer hall) is clad in Italian Carrara marble, hence its name, the Marble Temple. Inside, the stained glass depicts praying angels in a radical departure from tradition, in the material used and the treatment of the subjects.

Buddha Images

The Buddha image here is a superb copy of Phitsanulok's famed Phra Buddha Jinnarat, said to have wept tears of blood when Ayutthaya overran the northern town in the 14th century. Yet another striking departure from traditional architectural style is the temple's enclosed courtyard. Note also the temple's curved yellow Chinese roof tiles.

In the cloisters behind the *bot* (ordination hall), King Chulalongkorn placed copies of important Asian Buddha images to show his subjects the many ways in which the Buddha had been portrayed in Asia throughout history. Through the rear entrance of the

Left: Wat Pho's Reclining Buddha
Above: Buddha image, Marble Temple

Wat Benjamabophit and Vimanmek Mansion

400 m / 440 yds

- - - - Itinerary 3

Vimanmek
National Parliament
SUANSAT
Dusit Zoo
Anantha Samakhom (Throne Hall)
SUAN
DUSIT
Gate
Suan Kulab Palace
AMPORN
DUSIT
Statue of King Chulalongkorn
Parusakkawan Palace
Thanon Sri Ayutthaya
Wat Benjamabophit (Marble Temple)
Thanon Sri Ayutthaya
Gutis
Thanon Phitsanulok
Th. Ratchadamnoen Nok
Th. Thanon Pathon
Government House
Royal Turf Club
Khlong Prem Prachakon
Thanon Rama V

courtyard is a huge *bodhi* tree, approaching a century in age, which is reputed to be derived from the tree under which the Buddha gained enlightenment in India. Leave the temple through the northern door onto Sri Ayutthaya Road, turn left and keep going until you reach the next junction. Turn right into the broad plaza with its equestrian statue of King Chulalongkorn. Walk straight on and turn left towards **Ananta Samakhom Throne Hall** (daily 9.30am–3.15pm; admission fee), the former home of the Thai Parliament and originally built by Chulalongkorn in 1907 as his throne hall. Continue until you can see the National Parliament ahead and eventually Vimanmek, where the gate is signposted.

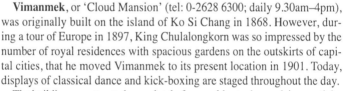

Vimanmek Mansion

At the entrance, present the same ticket from Wat Phra Kaew *(Itinerary 2)* or pay the small admission fee. Inside the lavish palace visitors must join a daily 45-minute guided tour in English; it is conducted free every half hour, beginning at 9.45am (last admission 2.45pm).

Vimanmek, or 'Cloud Mansion' (tel: 0-2628 6300; daily 9.30am–4pm), was originally built on the island of Ko Si Chang in 1868. However, during a tour of Europe in 1897, King Chulalongkorn was so impressed by the number of royal residences with spacious gardens on the outskirts of capital cities, that he moved Vimanmek to its present location in 1901. Today, displays of classical dance and kick-boxing are staged throughout the day.

The building, constructed completely from golden teak wood, is a pastiche of Thai, Italian and Victorian styles. The collection of objects and furniture is equally eclectic. Chulalongkorn was the first Siamese king to travel to the West and Vimanmek tells us what strange things caught his eye. The brass bathtub may have been the first of its kind in Siam. Note the array of small jewel-encrusted containers for storing betel leaves and areca nuts. Nowadays, Thais regard the chewing of these substances as repulsive, but

it seems to have been a principal pastime of Chulalongkorn's womenfolk. The photograph of the king on a visit to England surrounded by a dozen boys amuses many tourists. Yes, they were all his sons – and all about the same age. Chulalongkorn had about 40 concubines and twice as many children.

Wooden Museums

Some of the wooden houses in the grounds were the residences of favourite concubines, others were the homes of palace officials. These houses, including **Tamnak Ho** and **Suan Si Ruedu**, are now used as museums,

Above and left: Vimanmek Mansion
Right: Wang Suan Pakkad

each with its own delightful collection of period pieces. The **Royal Elephant Museum** is also within the grounds of Vimanmek, as well as a number of photographic museums. The **Abhisek Dusit Throne Hall** houses exquisite Thai handicrafts created by the Queen Sirikit-sponsored SUPPORT foundation. At the end of Vimanmek's west wing, on the edge of the *khlong* (canal), is a cluster of stilted wooden houses. The king had them built so that he could pretend to be a commoner. It is said that the king actually did the cooking himself and had his royal relatives wash the dishes.

4. WANG SUAN PAKKAD AND JIM THOMPSON HOUSE
(see map, p18–19)

Visit a Thai princess's palace in the morning and a silk king's traditional house in the afternoon, both built in classical Thai style.

Beat the traffic by taking the Skytrain to Phaya Thai BTS Station, then take a short walk or taxi ride to Wang Suan Pakkad.

Before the Thais eschewed wood for concrete, they evolved an architectural style all their own, one which blended into the tropical surroundings and took full advantage of the breezes. The following dwellings are two quite different examples of old-fashioned Thai homes.

Wang Suan Pakkad (Cabbage Patch Palace) is located at 352 Ayutthaya Road (tel: 0-2245 4934; daily 9am–4pm; admission fee). It was once the residence of Prince (1904–59) and Princess Chumbhot of Nakhon Sawan. However, it was Princess Chumbhot who was responsible for most of the work on the palace, which comprises five traditional teak wood structures. The palace was transported all the way from the north and erected around a pond.

Wander through the complex, pausing to look at the fine Ayutthaya-period manuscript cabinets, with their lacquer decorations and other items in the art collection. The princess was an avid collector of Ban Chiang pottery and Neolithic artefacts, housed in the back building on the right.

Suan Pakkad's centrepiece is the **Lacquer Pavilion**, one of the finest examples of priceless gold-and-black lacquer work in Asia. It has been reconstructed

from two monastic libraries and the interior walls are richly decorated with Buddhist scenes.

Thereafter, return to Phaya Thai BTS Station and take the train to **Siam BTS Station**. Easily accessed from the station are the malls of **Siam Centre**, **Siam Discovery Centre**, **Siam Paragon**, and **Mahboonkrong Shopping Centre** (MBK), which host numerous cafés and restaurants. Otherwise, change lines at Siam BTS Station and stop at **Ratchadamri BTS Station**, from where the deluxe **Four Seasons** (tel: 0-2250 1000) at 155 Ratchadamri Road, offering more lavish lunch options, is a stone's throw away. After lunch, take the train to **National Stadium BTS Station**. From here, take a short walk to **Jim Thompson House** on Soi Kasemsan 2.

A Silk King's House

The **Jim Thompson House** (tel: 0-2216 7368; daily 9am–5pm; admission fee; www.jimthompsonhouse.com), is an assemblage of six teak houses which create the archetypal Thai-style house. Built just after World War II, the house is stunning, with its peaceful garden setting and art collection. An American intelligence officer during the war, Jim Thompson made his fortune by introducing exotic Thai silk to the Western world. Thompson's life was as mysterious as his sudden disappearance – while out for an afternoon walk in the Malaysian jungle of Cameron Highlands in 1967. On the ground floor of the house are superb reproductions of old maps and wall hangings for sale. The admission fee includes a guided tour in English or French.

For a broader range of Jim Thompson silks, visit the large store (tel: 0-2632 8100) at 9 Surawong Road or its factory outlet (tel: 0-23326530) at 153 Sukhumvit Soi 93, where both fabrics and ready-made clothes are sold.

5. DAMNOEN SADUAK FLOATING MARKET AND THE ROSE GARDEN *(see map, p34)*

Journey by boat through the Damnoen Saduak Floating Market; visit the world's tallest Buddhist stupa; enjoy a cultural show, complete with elephants at the Rose Garden.

The easiest way to do this tour is on a package. A standard full-day tour begins with a hotel pick-up around 7am and heads 110km (70 miles) southwest of Bangkok. Most big hotels book through World Travel Service (tel: 0-2233 5900; www.wts-thailand.com), and tours cost 1,450 baht per person. A personal guide with a chauffeur-driven car costs around 9,000 baht per day.

Over the years, the popular **Damnoen Saduak Floating Market** (daily 7am–1pm) has outgrown several sites and moved further into the countryside of Ratchaburi Province. Nevertheless, it has lost little of its original appeal. The early start is designed to give you a jump on both the Bangkok traffic and the early-rising vendors, who begin paddling towards the market on their narrow *sampan* boats well before dawn. You will drive through the scenic Thonburi countryside, stopping along the way to photograph the **Samut Sakhon salt flats,** where windmills draw seawater for evaporation into table salt. At a boat landing, you board a longtail boat for a fast and exhilarating ride through the canals to the Damnoen Saduak Floating Market.

Floating Markets

There are actually three concentrated areas of floating markets, but most tours stop at **Talaat Hia Kui**, a parallel canal just south of Damnoen Saduak. If you are looking for souvenirs, there are plenty of shops in this area.

The floating market *(talaat naam)* is a Thai wonder, not only at Damnoen Saduak, but also in the hundreds of lush lowland canals and rivers throughout Thailand. Damnoen Saduak itself functions as a legitimate market and not one merely staged for tourists. Village women in their dark blue shirts and colourful *sarong* paddle *sampan* filled with fruits, spices, flowers, sweets and vegetables to trade either with buyers on land or with each other.

On some tours, the next stop is a snake farm, where the normally docile snakes are roused to action by handlers who virtually beat them. This offends many people, but be assured that this theatrical demonstration is not the normal practice at authentic snake farms. See the genuine show in Bangkok at the Snake Farm in Rama V Road, where snakes are bred for practical and medical purposes, and not commercial gain.

The tour continues to the town of **Nakhon Pathom** to see the colossal **Phra Pathom Chedi**, the world's tallest Buddhist stupa and the oldest such structure in Thailand. Originally dating back to 300 BC, the stupa was raised to its present height of 128m (420ft) by King Mongkut in 1860. However, his structure sadly collapsed in a rainstorm, and the one you see today was eventually completed by King Chulalongkorn. You can buy incense,

Left top: carving, Jim Thompson House
Left: exterior, Jim Thompson House
Right: Phra Pathom Chedi

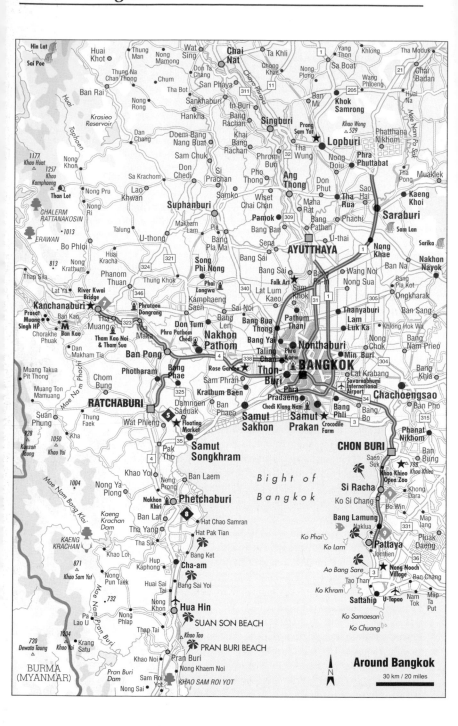

Around Bangkok

30 km / 20 miles

a candle and a lotus bud here and make a wish. Walk around the stupa, which rests on a circular terrace planted with trees that have associations with the life of the Buddha.

Rose Garden

Some 30km (20 miles) west of Bangkok is the much-visited **Rose Garden Country Resort** (daily 8am–6pm; admission fee; tel: 0-3432 2588; www.rose-garden.com) on the banks of the Ta Chin River. After lunch you will be taken to its **Thai Village** for a cultural show, where you will see a selection of everything that is considered to be typical of the culture of the country: folk dancing, Thai boxing, cockfighting, sword fighting, a wedding and a monk's ordination ceremony. This is followed by a demonstration of elephants at work and the chance to ride on an elephant for a small fee. Finally comes the long ride back through rush-hour traffic, arriving in Bangkok at about 7pm.

By this time, weary feet and empty stomachs will delight in the sci-fi-inspired **Bed Supperclub** (tel: 0-2651 3537; www.bedsupperclub.com) on Sukhumvit Soi 11, where diners can throw off their shoes and lounge on huge couches in an all-white cylindrical diner serving an exciting blend of Western and Thai food. Less than 50m (150ft) away, **Q Bar** (tel: 0-2252 3274) is the city's grooviest al fresco venue for late night drinks. For unsurpassable views, hit the 37th floor of the **Sofitel Silom**, where the chic **V9 bar** (daily 5pm–2am; tel: 0-2238 1991) overlooks the whole city. Some night owls may prefer the hot and heavy **Patpong** clubs 1km (½ mile) further up on Silom Road, around which a vast night market goes on until late.

Above: cultural show at Rose Garden
Right: risque Patpong nightlife

6. AYUTTHAYA *(see maps, p34 and below)*

The best way to approach the magnificent temples and palaces of the ancient Ayutthaya is as the first European explorers did in the 1660s: by boat along the Chao Phraya River. Be sure to include a sidetrip to the royal summer retreat of Bang Pa-In.

The Manohra Song, operated by Manohra Cruises (tel: 0-2477 0770; www.manohra cruises.com), has an expensive 3-day-2-night trip to Ayutthaya which departs from the pier at Bangkok Marriott Resort & Spa on Mondays and Thursdays. Another operator, the River Sun Cruise (tel: 0-2266 9125; www.riversuncruise. co.th), organises more affordable daily trips to Ayutthaya, leaving daily by air-conditioned coach from the River City Shopping Complex (23 Trok Rongnamkhaeng, Yota Road) at 8am and returning by the River Sun boat to Tha Si Phraya Pier (in front of the River City Shopping Complex) by about 4.30pm. A cheaper and more flexible option is to take the air-conditioned
bus (2 hours from the Northern Bus terminal) or train (3 hours from Hualam-phong station) for the 85-km (55-mile) trip to Ayutthaya. Alternatively, travel agents can organise similar tours by coach or a chauffeur-driven car.

A lesiurely cruise along the mighty Chao Phraya River to (or from) Ayut-thaya will allow you to witness the endless variety of activities that take place on this mighty waterway. Both the *Manohra Song* and *River Sun* include short tours of selected sights in Ayutthaya, with stops in **Bang Pa-In**, where

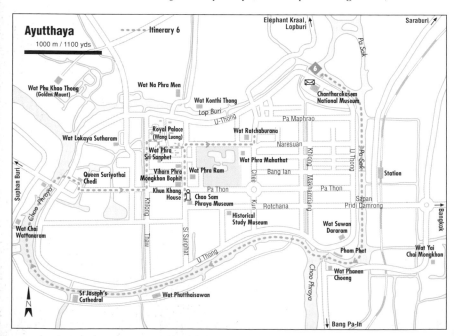

visitors disembark to see its charming collection of pavilions. Once used as a royal summer retreat by Thai kings, Bang Pa-In lies about 20km (12½ miles) south of the ruins of Ayutthaya.

The rulers of Ayutthaya used Bang Pa-In as long ago as the 17th century, but the buildings you see today date from the late 19th- and early 20th-century reigns of Rama IV (Mongkut) and Rama V (Chulalongkorn). The attractive palace built by King Mongkut is a mixture of classical Thai, Italian and Victorian styles. Only part of the royal quarters are opened to the public, but visitors can tour the opulent **Wehat Chamrun Palace**, a scarlet pavilion built in traditional Chinese style, adorned with delicate gold carvings and filled with a sumptuous collection of oriental *objets d'art*. Across the lawns lies a red and yellow striped tower; this is the **Withun Thatsana** observatory tower. It's possible to climb up to the top to gain a bird's eye views of the surrounding countryside as well as the topiary garden below, where children can romp among the well-pruned 'elephants'. A Thai-style pavilion called the **Aisawan Thippaya-at**, in the middle of the adjacent lake, is regarded as one of the finest examples of traditional architecture in Thailand.

Ayutthaya

If you opt for the *Manohra Song* or *River Sun* cruises, expect an abbreviated tour of the temples, palaces and museums of **Ayutthaya Historical Park** (daily 8am–6.30pm; admission fee). Organising your own tour with an overnight stay in Ayutthaya will allow more time for an in-depth and leisurely tour of the sights.

Ayutthaya, situated 76km (48 miles) upstream from Bangkok. was founded in 1351 by Prince U-thong, who later become King Ramathibodi I. By the 15th century, the kingdom of Sukhothai had passed under Ayutthayan rule, and the court's influence spread as far as Angkor in the east, and Pegu, in Burma (Myanmar), to the west. Regular relations with Europe began in the early 1500s with the Portuguese, and later with the Dutch, British, and especially the French. Europeans wrote awed accounts of the fabulous wealth of the courts of Ayutthaya and of its 2,000 temple spires clad in gold.

Ayutthaya was one of the richest cities in Asia by the 1600s and, with a population of one million, greater than that of contemporary London. Merchants came from Europe, the Middle East and elsewhere in Asia to trade in its markets. As quickly as Ayutthaya rose, it collapsed. Burmese armies had been battering at its gates for centuries, and finally, in 1767, they triumphed, burning and looting Ayutthaya without restraint and destroying most of the city's monuments in the process. Within a year, Ayutthaya had become a ghost town, its population reduced to a few thousands.

Ayutthaya is situated on an island at the junction of three rivers, the Chao Phraya, Pa Sak and Lop Buri. The ruins stand by themselves on the western half of the island, with modern Ayutthaya, a bustling town in the eastern part.

Left top: Bang Pa-In, former Summer Palace
Right: ruins of an Ayutthayan stupa

Ayutthaya's Highlights

Described below are some of the highlights of Ayutthaya, which can be done by a combination of longtail boat, on foot and by *tuk-tuk* if you are travelling independently. Close by the boat pier, where longtail boats can be hired for trips around the island, is **Chantharakasem National Museum** (Wed–Sun 9am–4pm; admission fee), formerly known as the Chantharakasem Palace. It was originally constructed outside the city walls, close to the confluence of the rivers and the canal. King Maha Thammaracha built it for his son Prince Naresuan (later king), and it became the residence for future heirs apparent. In 1767, the Burmese destroyed the palace, but King Mongkut resurrected it in the 19th century as a royal summer retreat for escaping the lowland heat. Today, it looks out on the noisiest part of modern Ayutthaya. The palace's collection isn't that impressive but it still worthy of a perusal.

Across the street from the palace is the night market with food stalls set up beside the water every evening. It's a good spot to eat cheap local food and unwind at the end of the day.

Further south is **Wat Suwan Dararam**, a temple constructed near the end of the Ayutthayan period. The foundations of the *bot* dip in the centre, in emulation of the graceful deck line of a boat. This typical Ayutthayan decoration is meant to suggest a boat that carries pious Buddhists to salvation. Delicately carved columns support the roof, and the interior walls are decorated with brilliantly-coloured frescoes. To the southeast is **Wat Yai Chai Mongkhon**, originally established in the mid-1300s. The large stupa, built to match the Phu Khao Thong Pagoda just north of Ayutthaya, was erected in celebration of King Naresuan's victory over the Burmese in 1592.

Close to the confluence of the Pa Sak and Chao Phraya rivers stands **Wat Phanan Choeng**. This temple was established 26 years before Ayutthaya's foundation was laid, and houses a huge seated Buddha. Wat Phanan Choeng was a favourite with Chinese traders, who would come here to pray before setting out on long voyages; the temple still retains an unmistakably Chinese atmosphere.

Ayutthaya was at one time surrounded by solid ramparts 20m (65ft) high and 5m (16ft) thick, only portions of which remain. One of the best-preserved sections is at **Phom Phet**, across the river from Wat Phanan Choeng. West of Wat Phanan Choeng and further upstream, the quiet and seldom visited **Wat Phutthaisawan** stands on the riverbank. Continuing slightly further upstream, the restored **Cathedral of St Joseph** is a Catholic reminder of the large European population that lived in the city at its prime. As the river bends to the north, note one of Ayutthaya's most romantic ruins, **Wat Chai Wattanaram**, erected in 1630. The *prang* (spire), with its surrounding stupa and rows of headless Buddhas make a fine contrast to the restored **Queen Suriyothai Chedi** on the city side of the river. Legend has it that, dressed as a man, the

Left: Wat Phra Sri Sanphet's Buddha image

valiant Ayutthayan queen rode her elephant into battle beside her husband, King Mahachakkraphat (1548–69). When she saw him attacked by a Burmese prince, Queen Suriyothai moved her elephant between them and received the lance blow intended for her husband. The lance blow proved fatal and Queen Suriyothai became one of Thailand's greatest heroines in the process.

Disembark from your longtail boat near Queen Suriyothai Chedi and follow Pa Thon Road to the east until you come to the junction with Khlong Thaw Road; then head north to the old palace of **Wang Luang** (Royal Palace).

Wang Luang was of substantial size in its heyday, if the foundations for the stables of 100 elephants are any indication. Sadly, only remnants of the foundations survive to mark the site. Close by are the three stupa of **Wat Phra Sri Sanphet**, a royal temple built in 1491 to honour three 15th-century kings. The identical stupa have been restored and stand in contrast to the surrounding ruins. For two centuries after Ayutthaya's fall, a huge bronze Buddha sat unsheltered near Wat Phra Sri Sanphet. Based on the original, a new building, the **Viharn Phra Mongkhon Bophit**, was built in 1956 around the restored statue.

To the east of Viharn Phra Mongkhon Bophit stands the **Wat Phra Ram** (daily 8am–5pm; admission fee), one of Ayutthaya's oldest temples. Constructed in 1369 by the son of Ayutthaya's founder, its buildings have been completely restored twice. Elephant gates punctuate the old walls, and the central terrace is dominated by a crumbling *prang* (spire) to which clings a gallery of stucco *naga* (serpents), *garuda* (birds) and various statues of the Buddha.

Across the lake are two of Ayutthaya's finest temples. Built in 1424 by the seventh king of Ayutthaya as a memorial to his brothers, **Wat Ratchaburana** (daily 8am–5pm; admission fee) dominates its surroundings. Art works found here are now kept in the **Chao Sam Phraya Museum** (Wed–Sun 9am–4pm; admission fee) to the south. The beautiful **Wat Phra Mahathat** (daily 8am–6pm; admission fee), found across the road from Wat Ratchaburana, dates from the 1380s. Its huge *prang* originally stood 46m (150ft) high. Look out for the stone Buddha faces, each a metre (3ft) in height, which stand proudly around the ruins.

Further afield, a little way north of Ayutthaya, **Wat Phu Khao Thong** (Golden Mount), stands with its 80-m (260-ft)-high stupa. Climb to its upper terraces to take in a panoramic view of the countryside. The temple dates from 1387. In 1957, to mark 2,500 years of Buddhism, a 2½-kg (5½-lb) ball, cast in sold gold, was mounted on top of the stupa.

Above: Wat Phra Ram

7. KANCHANABURI AND THE RIVER KWAI BRIDGE
(see map, p34)

Journey to the memorable River Kwai Bridge and Kanchanaburi war cemeteries; travel along the only remaining section of the original 'Death Railway' between Kanchanaburi and Nam Tok; you may want to stay in the Kanchanaburi area, where you can go swimming, hiking or rafting.

Kanchanaburi, 129km (81 miles) away from the capital, can be reached by bus, or train from Hualamphong Station or Bangkok Noi Station. Departing only on Sunday, Saturday and public holidays, the Hualamphong service leaves at 6.30am and arrives in Kanchanaburi at 10am, giving you a few hours to see the bridge, Nam Tok and the Allied War Cemeteries before departing at 5pm and arriving back in Bangkok around 7.30pm. The Bangkok Noi Station offers more frequent daily services to Kanchanaburi. Air-conditioned buses leave daily from the Southern Bus Terminal every 15 minutes from 5.30am until 7.30pm. The trip takes 2–3 hours. Alternatively, travel agents in Bangkok can organise similar tours by air-conditioned coach or a chauffeur-driven car.

The train's first stop is **Nakhon Pathom** at around 7.55am, where it waits for about 40 minutes to allow you to see **Phra Pathom Chedi** *(Itinerary 5)*, the world's tallest Buddhist monument, standing at 128m (420ft). It then continues through the countryside to **Kanchanaburi**, in the Mae Klong Valley.

Construction of the infamous 'Death Railway' began during the Japanese occupation of Thailand and Burma in World War II in an attempt to shorten supply lines between Japan and Burma. The Japanese were brutal taskmasters in a harsh landscape. A combination of hard labour, regular beatings, disease and malnutrition led to the deaths of 16,000 of the 61,000 Allied POWs and about 100,000 of the estimated 250,000 conscripted Asian labourers. As one author grimly noted, such figures amounted to a 'life for every sleeper'.

Above: the infamous Bridge on River Kwai

For a large part of its 400km (250 miles), the railway ran parallel with the Khwae Noi. 'Khwae' (more accurate than 'Kwai'), is a designation rather than a name; it means 'branch of the Mae Klong River'. There are two branches, the Khwae Noi (Small) and the Khwae Yai (Large).

The River Kwai Bridge

The critical bridge, made famous in print and film, was located at Tha Makham, outside Kanchanaburi. An early wooden version was destroyed by Allied bombing in 1943, only to be replaced by steel spans brought from Indonesia by the Japanese. This too was destroyed by bombing and only repaired after the war, when two new steel spans were erected. This segment of the railway still functions and is known as the **'Bridge on the River Kwai'** (it actually spans the larger Khwae Yai).

Today, the bridge stands mainly as a pilgrimage site. The train stops so you can walk across it. The pedestrian walkway over the bridge is not as precarious as it looks; niches between the original curved spans provide a refuge in case a train happens to come along. Try to look beyond the current commercialisation of the area and, instead, visualise the difficult conditions in which the POWs toiled. Just south of the bridge, exhibits at the **Thailand-Burma Railway Centre** (tel: 0-3451 0067; daily 9am–5pm; admission fee) provide further detail on the history of the Death Railway and even include a full-scale replica of the original wooden bridge.

The train then continues over the creaking wooden tracks – all that remains of the original 'Death Railway' – through jungle along the base of a tall limestone cliff, before ending at the terminus at **Nam Tok**. You have two hours at Nam Tok for a delicious Thai lunch, a swim in the pond below the waterfall or a walk in the jungle.

The train returns to **Kanchanaburi**, where you can visit the two war cemeteries, the final resting place of the Allied POWs who died building the infamous railway. The **Kanchanaburi Allied War Cemetery**, just off Chaokunen Road in the north-central part of town, is the more easily accessible of the two. The **Chung Kai Allied War Cemetery** is situated on the west bank of the Khwae Noi, so a short ferry trip and a longish walk are required to reach it. The **JEATH War Museum** (daily 8.30am–6pm; admission fee) – the letters denoting the countries involved in its construction: Japan, England, America/Australia, Thailand and Holland – was constructed to resemble the bamboo huts in which the POWs lived. Set up in 1977, utensils, paintings, writings and other objects donated by prisoners recall some of the horror of their hell-like existence.

If time permits, stay several days in Kanchanaburi, hiking in the bamboo forests, rafting down the river and sleeping in houseboats. In late November and early December, the town holds a series of popular *son-et-lumières* centred on the bridge. You could also travel to the **Three Pagodas Pass** on the Burmese border.

Right: Allied War Cemetery

8. PHETCHABURI AND HUA HIN *(see map, p34)*

Journey by train to Phetchaburi with its ancient temples and the remains of King Mongkut's early 19th-century palace, then head on towards Thailand's royal resort town of Hua Hin.

The train from Bangkok's Hualamphong Station takes 3 hours to get to Phetchaburi and another hour to Hua Hin. If Hua Hin, 160km (100 miles) south of Bangkok, is your chief destination, you can catch a bus from Bangkok's Southern Bus Terminal. It takes about 3½ hours to get there by bus, while a private car with driver takes slightly less time. Alternatively, a taxi ride, taking about 3 hours, can be negotiated for a flat rate of 1,500–2,000 baht.

Phetchaburi is 125km (78 miles) southwest of Bangkok. It is famed for its historical park, **Phra Nakhon Khiri** – 'Hill of the Holy City'. The hill, also known as **Khao Wang** (tel: 0-3240 1006; daily 8.30am–3pm), rises over the town and is studded with temples and the remains of King Mongkut's early 19th-century palace. Built as a retreat by King Mongkut, it has recently been restored.

A cable car ascends the northern flank of the hill, eliminating the arduous climb, but you must hire a minibus to get to and from the train station. A steep path lined with fragrant frangipani trees leads past the elephant stables to the main halls, which combine European and Chinese architectural styles. Towering above the other buildings of the complex is an observatory where the king indulged in a passion for astronomy. If you are walking up the hill, do be wary of the monkeys that live there as they have been known to bite.

Phetchaburi has four temples worthy of a visit. **Wat Yai Suwannaram** (daily 8am–6pm; free) is east of the river, and **Wat Kamphaeng Laeng** (daily 8am–6pm; free), just southeast of it. Wat Yai Suwannaram, built in the 17th century, holds murals that are among the oldest in the country. Note

Above: King Mongkut's palace at Khao Wang

the lovely old library building on stilts in the middle of the pond – this was an early method for protecting manu-scripts from termites. Wat Kamphaeng Laeng, a Khmer temple, is thought to delineate the most westerly frontier of the Angkorian Empire. **Wat Mahathat** (daily 8am–6pm; free), in the middle of town, is marked by a huge *prang* (spire) that towers over it. Much of the decor is new, but it nevertheless acts as a magnet for Buddhists, and visitors will find that festivals are often in progress there.

Some 5km (3 miles) north of town is **Khao Luang Cave** (daily 8am–6pm; admission fee), easily reached by motorcycle taxi or *songthaew* (pick-up truck). The huge cave holds dozens of Buddha images, and stalactites hang from the ceiling. Two holes in the ceiling of the cave enable sunlight to penetrate around midday, creating an ethereal scene.

Hua Hin and Pranburi Beaches

Catch the evening train from Phetchaburi station to **Hua Hin**. Regular buses and taxis ferry between the railway station and beach resorts in Hua Hin. For half a century, Hua Hin has reigned as Thailand's royal playground. King Bhumibol's palace is located on the northern end of the beach but is out of bound to visitors. In the last two years, Hua Hin's new luxury hotels and smaller resorts further south near **Pranburi** have become fashionable weekend retreats for harried city dwellers. On the beach, you can rent catamarans, windsurf boards, parasails and water-skiing equipment. Hua Hin town

has good fresh seafood restaurants and a bustling night market for souvenirs and local snacks.

In addition to the big name chain resorts are world-class golf courses such as the **Royal Hua Hin Golf Course** (Damnoenkasem Road; tel: 0-3251 2475) and the spectacular Jack Niklaus-designed course at **Springfield Royal Country Club** (193 Huay-Sai Nua, Petchkasem Road, Cha-Am; tel: 0-3247 1303).

Hua Hin also boasts a number of internationally acclaimed spas offering day spa facilities as well as resi-

Above: Khao Luang Cave
Left: Hua Hin beach

bangkok & environs

dential programmes for those serious about getting fit, detoxifying or just simply chilling out for a week or two. The historic but stylish **Sofitel Central Hua Hin** (tel: 0-3251 2021; www.sofitel.com) has been joined by the modern **Hyatt** (tel: 0-3252 1234; huahin.regency.hyatt.com), **Hilton** (tel: 0-3253 8999; www.hilton.com) and **Marriott** (tel: 0-3251 1881; www.marriott.com) on the main beach. The **Anantara Resort and Spa** (tel: 0-3252 0250; www.anantara.com) is one of Hua Hin's best appointed hotels. Boasting both a beach front and lush tropical gardens, it has spacious lagoon rooms overlooking lily ponds. Its **Mandara Spa** is recognised as one of the region's best.

Chiva-Som (tel: 0-3253 6536; www.chivasom.com) and **Evason Hua Hin** (tel: 0-3263 2111; www.evasonresorts.com) are two more first-rate spa resorts further south. The former is famous for holistic health regimes catering to well-heeled hedonists, while the Evason has superb accommodations and a chic courtyard spa offering a wide range of Thai and Swedish treatments.

For those willing to drive 35km (21½ miles) further on to Pranburi, the 10-suite **Aleenta** (tel: 0-3257 0194; www.aleenta.com) offers small-scale designer luxury on a secluded beach. Its rooms and villas have a contemporary Thai-Mediterranean feel and a range of traditional Thai spa treatments are available.

9. SI RACHA AND PATTAYA *(see map, p34)*

Take a short break from the bustle of Bangkok and head east towards the nearby beaches of Ko Si Chang and Pattaya for a little sun, sea and watersports as well as wonderful seafood meals.

Regular air-conditioned buses leave Bangkok's Eastern Bus Terminal for Si Racha and Pattaya. Si Racha is around a 2-hour (105km/65 miles) drive via the expressway through Chonburi, while Pattaya is slightly more than 30 minutes (40km/25 miles) further.

So far largely overlooked by Western visitors, but overwhelmingly popular with Thais, is the small fishing town of **Si Racha**. If you want a break from Bangkok but don't fancy the bright lights or sleaze of Pattaya, this is a good (and relatively inexpensive) alternative, with excellent seafood. Some 45 minutes away by ferry is the island of Ko Si Chang, with its sandy beaches, several of which are pristine and secluded. Ferries leave Si Racha for the island on a regular basis throughout the day.

East of Si Racha, off Highway 3241, the **Sriracha Tiger Zoo** (tel: 0-3829 6556; www.tigerzoo.com; daily 8am–6pm; admission fee) boasts the largest collection of tigers in the world. It's a good place to take children to, as, apart from tigers, there are a number of other animals on the site.

Continue for just another 40km (25 miles) along Sukhumvit Road (Highway 3) and you will arrive at one of Thailand's major tourist destinations – the infamous beach resort of Pattaya.

Infamous Pattaya Beach

Not so long ago, the holiday resort of **Pattaya** was just a small fishing village on the eastern shore of the Gulf of Thailand. Then it was 'discovered' and began its rapid

Left: tiger at Sriracha Tiger Zoo

development into one of Asia's major resorts. It is now a small city, popular with foreign visitors and Bangkok weekenders alike. There is no doubt that Pattaya is brash, loud and garish. It has more bars, discos and massage parlours, not to mention prostitutes, than Bangkok but there are also decent beaches, sightseeing opportunities and an array of watersports – all at prices

lower than Phuket. Pattaya is trying to change its image from that of an all-night party town to a family resort – but it still has a long way to go.

Pattaya proper starts at the Dolphin roundabout. At this end of Pattaya – and as far as Central Road – are many first-class hotels set in tropical gardens: Dusit Resort, Orchid Lodge, the boat-shaped Royal Cruise, Ramada Beach, Montien and Nipa Lodge are among the most prominent. In the same area are a number of excellent restaurants and shopping precincts lining Second Road, and some parts of Beach Road. On Second Road are situated the most important of the huge entertainment complexes of the city, **Tiffany**, **Alcazar** and the **Palladium**.

From Central Road to South Road is the busy commercial heart of the city, augmented by numerous hotels. There are many restaurants too, perhaps the best-known being **Ruen Thai** (485/3 Pattaya 2 Road; tel: 0-3842 5911), where in a magical setting of palms, orchids and fountains, you can dine on superb Thai food and watch classical Thai dancing.

South Pattaya is divided into two. Between Pratumnak Road and Beach Road South is the nightlife heart of the city. Here, the seemingly endless assemblage of go-go bars, clubs and cabarets are served by dozens of excellent restaurants, some set on piers over the water. Seafood is the main theme, but there is scarcely a cuisine not represented here. This is Pattaya's **'Golden Mile'**, always busy, often great fun, but often rather seedy as well.

Beyond Tappraya Road, it's much quieter. **Khao Pratumnak** (Palace Hill) rises above the flat land of the rest of the town, topped by the huge golden Buddha of **Wat Khao Phra Yai**, gazing out over the headland between the bay of Pattaya and Jomtien beach. There is a splendid viewpoint over the whole city to the green hills beyond. Nestled on the cliffs or down on the beaches by the headland of Laem Pattaya is another cluster of first-class hotels, rivalling those of North Pattaya.

Finally, there is the southern section of Pattaya, with its long **Jomtien** beach, stretching southwards for several kilometres and dotted with deck chairs and umbrellas. The beachfront has been encroached by development but only a short way inland the country is still untouched: palms, fields, marshland and temples.

Above: Pattaya's Dusit Resort
Right: Jomtien beach

bangkok & environs

North Thailand

When the Central Plains begin to swelter, many Thais flee to the North to enjoy the cooler temperatures and green hills. The region, isolated from Bangkok until the arrival of the railway in the 1920s, developed its own culture, one heavily influenced by Lao art and, in part, by Burmese traditions. The result is a wealth of ornate teak or stucco-covered temples quite unlike those found elsewhere in Thailand, and unique crafts like silverwork, woodcarving and umbrella making. Prior to the 20th century, the North existed as an independent kingdom called Lanna, or the 'Kingdom of a Million Rice Fields'.

Chiang Mai, the capital of the North, is regarded as the cultural heart of Thailand with numerous workshops creating a variety of wood, ceramic and lacquer artefacts, as well as other crafts. The city, founded seven centuries ago by King Mengrai the Great, has remained the cultural and political centre of the North from the time of the Lanna Kingdom through to the present day.

Chiang Mai, easily accessed by plane and train from Bangkok *(see page 93)*, is for the more adventurous traveller. Visitors normally spend a few days exploring the temples and the markets and then head into the hills to trek to hill tribe villages, ride elephants through the jungles, and float down rivers on bamboo rafts. Chiang Mai also serves as the gateway to ancient kingdoms like Lamphun, Lampang, Chiang Rai and Chiang Saen, and picturesque towns like Mae Hong Son, Mae Salong, Chom Thong and others. Buses serve these outer areas but those preferring independent travel can opt to rent jeeps or motorcycles for their journeys. There are hotels, guesthouses and restaurants in each of the main towns.

Finally, to the south of the old Lanna kingdom lies the equally ancient historical site of Sukhothai, the capital of the first Thai kingdom. Sukhothai, regarded as the cradle of Thai civilisation, began around 1238, when King Sri Intradit asserted his independence from the Khmer Empire. Eventually, it grew to include most of modern-day Thailand and parts of the Malay Peninsula and Burma, and is synonymous with some of the finest artistic endeavours in Thai history, including exquisite Buddha images.

In reading the following itineraries, please note that 'H' means 'Highway Number' (ie 'H108' means 'Highway 108'). Similarly, 'KM' refers to the number painted on the roadside kilometre posts. *Itineraries 10, 11* and *12* can be followed by making Chiang Mai your base and using local transport to get around. *Itinerary 13*, Sukhothai, can be visited from either Bangkok or Chiang Mai by Bangkok Airways, air-conditioned bus, or train. Chiang Rai makes a pleasant base for *Itinerary 14* and to visit Mae Hong Son *(Itinerary 15)*. The quickest option is to take the short 40-minute hop on Bangkok Airways from Chiang Mai.

Left: Mae Hong Son's lush landscape
Right: *naga* (serpent) at Wat Chedi Luang

10. CHIANG MAI'S HIGHLIGHTS *(see map below)*

Explore four old monasteries by trishaw, ascend a sacred mountain, visit a Hmong village and a royal palace. Then enjoy a riverside dinner and indulge in some nighttime shopping.

There are frequent plane and train connections between Bangkok and Chiangmai (see page 93). For this itinerary, flag down either a samlor

(pedal trishaw) or a tuk-tuk. Hire the driver for about 3 hours and visit the old city of Chiang Mai. Alternatively, keen walkers can cover the 4-km (2½-mile) morning route on foot, or hire a bicycle for a half day.

Before you start exploring Chiang Mai, start the day with a hearty breakfast. Have it at your hotel or ride a trishaw to **Riverview Lodge** (25 Charoen Prathet Road; tel: 0-5327 1109/10) for breakfast in a riverside garden. Then begin what will be a long but interesting day visiting the temples of Wat Chedi Luang, Wat Pan Tao, Wat Phra Singh and Wat Chiang Mun.

Wat Chedi Luang

The sheer size of **Wat Chedi Luang** (daily 8am–6pm) makes it one of Chiang Mai's most imposing and beautiful temples. Step through the entrance gate from Phra Pokklao Road, and note the tall gum tree on the left. Legend has it that when the tree falls, so will the city of Chiang Mai. Shaded by its boughs is a city pillar similar to those

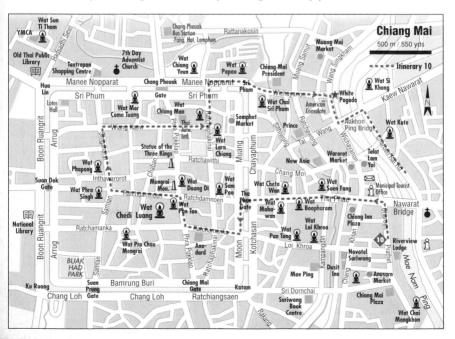

that mark the geographic centre of most Thai towns; its guardian spirit is said to watch over the city's inhabitants.

The temple's most remarkable structure is the huge stupa at the rear. Built in 1401 by King Saeng Muang Ma, in 1454 it was raised to 86m (282ft) by King Tilokaraja, builder of Wat Jet Yot. A massive earthquake in 1545 shattered the upper portion, reducing it to 42m (138ft). Its superstructure was never rebuilt, but the base and reliquary have been impressively restored. Exit Chedi Luang, walk down the street and enter the first gateway on the left to **Wat Pan Tao** (daily 8am–6pm). Its teak *viharn* (prayer hall) with its crimson pillars and golden peacock framed by golden serpents is a masterpiece of Lanna art. The interior is less interesting but still worth examining.

Even from a distance, **Wat Phra Singh** (daily 8am–6pm), the best example of Lanna-style architecture, is outstanding. Situated at the T-junction of Ratchdamnoen and Singharat roads, its *viharn* is superbly proportioned with a front wall decorated in gold flowers on a red lacquer background. Like many Lanna temples, its balustrade is a *naga* (serpent) with a *makara* (mythical water beast) emerging from its mouth, a motif found in many Cambodian monuments. Inside the temple, murals depict the life of the Buddha before he came to earth and achieved enlightenment.

Leave the *viharn* and turn left to the beautiful *ho trai* (monastic library) with its tranquil stucco angels. Running at right angles behind the *viharn* is a beautiful wooden *bot* (ordination hall) with a superb stucco and gold entrance. Behind it is an elephant-supported stupa built by King Pha Yu in 1345 to hold the ashes of his father, King Kam Fu.

The most beautiful of Wat Phra Singh's building is the famous **Phra Viharn Laikram** to the left of the stupa. As with all *bot*, its sacred boundary is defined by six *bai sema* (boundary stones). Although built in 1811, it embodies the finest Lanna architectural traditions. Intricately carved stucco door frames compete in beauty with the doors themselves. Inside, 19th-century murals on the right wall tell the story of Saengthong, the Prince of the Golden Conch, a mythical Thai hero. The left wall is devoted to Suphannahong, a mythical swan seen frequently in Northern art and architecture.

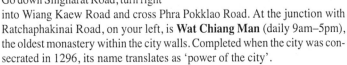

Sacred Power

Go down Singharat Road, turn right into Wiang Kaew Road and cross Phra Pokklao Road. At the junction with Ratchaphakinai Road, on your left, is **Wat Chiang Man** (daily 9am–5pm), the oldest monastery within the city walls. Completed when the city was consecrated in 1296, its name translates as 'power of the city'.

Its central building, a 19th-century Lanna-style *viharn* is decorated with the three-headed elephant god, Erawan. Look for the superbly carved teak

Left top: Wat Chedi Luang
Right: stone elephants support Wat Chiang Man

gable panels. Inside are several handsome bronze Buddha images from the Lanna and U-thong (15th-century) periods. Ask a monk to unlock the doors. The murals of the right-hand *viharn* chronicle Buddha's life with the *chadoks* (previous incarnations of the Buddha) appearing in the lower panels. The altar holds Chiang Mai's two most sacred Buddha images: the small crystal **Phra Setang Khamani** on the left, dating back to 1281, brings rain and protects the city from fire; the finely carved **Phra Sila** on the right was reputedly brought from India around AD1000.

Walk to the rear of the compound. Reflecting Sri Lankan influences, the 15th-century stupa appears to be supported by 15 brick and stucco elephants, an architectural device found in several Sukhothai and Kamphaeng Phet stupa. Left of the stupa is the *ho trai*, a masterpiece of Thai wood carving and lacquer decoration. In its small museum are lacquer manuscript cabinets, Buddha images, pipes, and old Thai money. In the far left-hand corner of the courtyard, the plain wooden doors of the *bot* open onto some superb Lanna and U-thong period bronze Buddha images.

Your last trishaw stop is the **Gallery Bar & Restaurant** (25-9 Charoenrat Road; tel: 0-5324 8601), decorated with artefacts from Lanna culture. Here you can enjoy an exquiste Thai lunch by the banks of the Ping River.

Sacred Mountain

The afternoon takes you up **Doi Suthep**, the city's most sacred mountain. Minibuses to Doi Suthep and Phuping leave from Tha Phae Road in front of the Bangkok Bank every 10 minutes. They climb the long and winding

road from the western end of Huai Kaew Road just past the zoo. If you go by car, drive 12km (7½ miles) to the car park of Wat Doi Suthep, but instead of stopping, continue up the road on the left through pine forests to Phuping, 4km (2½ miles) further on.

Phuping Palace, the royal family's Chiang Mai residence, is a command post for development projects in Northern Thai and hill tribe villages. When the royal family is not in residence, the beautiful flower gardens are opened for viewing (tel: 0-5321 9932; Sat–Sun and holidays 8.30am–4pm; admission fee). Continue another 3km (1½ miles) to the Hmong village of **Doi Pui**. The village seems to be little more than a hill tribe theme park. Two small museums are found in the village, one devoted to the cultivation of opium and the other to hill tribe implements. If you feel uncomfortable with the prospect of visiting a 'human zoo', ask your guide to bypass the village. Note: Hmong tribes expect payment for all photographs.

Above: Phuping, the royal family's residence
Right top: stupa at Wat Phra That Doi Suthep
Right: Chang Khlan handicraft shop

An Elephant's Choice

Return to **Wat Phra That Doi Suthep** (daily 8am–6pm), Chiang Mai's most famous temple. A funicular railway carries you to the summit but resist the temptation to ride it. You accumulate more merit (and a healthy workout) by climbing the 210 steps (304 if you count from the car park). Legend says that a monk named Sumana placed half of a Buddha relic on an elephant's back and set it loose; wherever the elephant stopped, a temple would be built to house the gem. That elephant must have had a perverse streak, because it began climbing Doi Suthep until it reached a height of 1,073m (3,521ft). It is here that Wat Phra That Doi Suthep was built.

Remove your shoes and climb to the inner sanctuary. Shorts are taboo but vendors near the entrance rent sarongs. The upper courtyard is highlighted by a dazzling gilded brass stupa which gleams in the afternoon sun. Small gilded Buddha images cap the spiked fence pickets and peer from odd corners. Framed photographs honour a long-deceased rooster which would peck at the feet of ignorant tourists who entered the courtyard wearing shoes. At 5pm, monks gather in the western *viharn* to chant their prayers. After listening to the ethereal chanting, leave the courtyard and turn left. Strike the big bronze bells for good luck and walk to the balustrade to watch dusk descend on Chiang Mai far below.

Return to your hotel, and after freshening up, head for the elegant **Le Grand Lanna** (San Kampaeng Road; tel: 0-5326 2569), which serves delicious Lanna cuisine in a wooden building amidst ponds and open-air pavilions. After dinner, take a *tuk-tuk* to either **Chang Khlan Night Market** (daily 5–11pm) for a spot of handicraft shopping or the charming **Vila Cini** (30-4 Charoenrat Road, tel: 0-5324 6246), a silk and antiques emporium set in a 140-year-old shophouse. Next door, **Oriental Style** (daily 8am–11pm) sells a wide range of superb homeware, accessories and crafts.

north thailand

11. BORSANG HANDICRAFT TOUR *(see pullout map)*

Spend a morning observing how Thai artisans create some of Chiang Mai's exquisite handicrafts.

Hire a tuk-tuk for this morning shopping tour. Head east out of town on the Charoen Muang Road, until you meet the Super Highway.

You will be visiting a variety of shops on the road to **Borsang**, all of which will welcome you in to watch craftsmen create the art objects for which Chiang Mai is famed. As you will quickly discover, the range of items is quite broad, although the quality varies according to the individual craftsman. Wander around at will – each shop has a showroom and you are under no obligation to buy. If an item does take your fancy, the shop can arrange air or sea shipping at reasonable rates. The following craft shops are strung out along the 9-km (5½-mile) road from Chiang Mai to Borsang beginning at the Super Highway junction.

Lacquerware and Wood

Napa Lacquerware (tel: 0-5343 0436) is at 8/2 San Kampaeng Road (KM3.2). Northern lacquerware involves gold leaf designs on glossy black, or green and black designs on a dark red base. Items such as betel boxes, serving trays and jewellery boxes are created from bamboo and overlaid with lacquer. Napa also covers its containers in crushed, dyed eggshell mosaics. Among the most popular items are the gold and black lacquer boxes (check carefully to ensure that the design is cleanly rendered).

   The **Pon Art Gallery** (tel: 0-5333 8361), 35/3 Moo 3, San Kampaeng Road (KM5.8), comprises a number

Above: Chiang Mai's famous umbrellas
Right: woodcarver's tools

of Thai-style houses crammed with an astounding variety of Thai and Burmese wooden gods and whimsical beasts which are ideal as decorative items. The neo-antiques sold here are produced in Baan Tawai, a small village south of Chiang Mai near Hang Dong (which is worth a side trip). Even if you have no desire to own a mirror-mosaic dragon or a red Ganesh elephant god, it is fun to browse for an hour or two at this interesting shop.

Silver and Other Stuff

Lannathai Silver (tel: 0-5333 8015/7), 79 Moo 3, San Kamphaeng Road (KM6.1), produces both antique and modern silverware and hill tribe jewellery. The silver content is low but the workmanship is good and the variety of items and prices ensure you will find a small gift to your liking.

Shinawatra (tel: 0-5333 8053/5) is at 145/1–2 San Kamphaeng Road (KM7.1). Observe how silkworms fed on mulberry leaves produce filaments that are woven into Thai silk and tailored into garments. The air-conditioned showroom carries printed silk items like scarves and pillowcases. It also sells Thai silk in lengths to be cut into suits and gowns by tailors in Chiang Mai and Bangkok.

Chamchuree Lapidary (tel: 0-5333 8631), 166/1 San Kamphaeng Road (KM7.5), carves Burmese jade into pendants and jewellery. The nephrite and jadeite comes from across the border in Burma; you save money by being so near to the source. **Arts & Crafts Chiang Mai** (tel: 0-5333 8026), 172 Moo 2, San Kamphaeng Road (KM7.8), casts bronze deities and animals which can be used indoors and outdoors.

Chiang Mai Sudaluck (tel: 0-5333 8006), 99/9 San Kamphaeng Road (KM8.2), carves Northern timber into furniture and home decor items. Ranging from beds and writing desks to chopping boards and trivets, a range of natural and glossy finishes are offered. A lightly brushed painted style which gives an antique look is the most popular.

The **Umbrella Making Centre** (tel: 0-5333 8324), 111/2 San Kamphaeng Road (KM9), combines bamboo, string and *sah* paper (made from the bark of the paper mulberry tree) into umbrellas that are a marvel of engineering. This is Chiang Mai's most famous product and ranges in size from parasols to huge patio umbrellas, and in decorative styles ranging from plain to outrageously ornate.

Prempracha's Collection (tel: 0-5333 8857), 224 San Kamphaeng Road at the Borsang intersection (KM9), skilfully moulds celadon, ceramic, blue and white porcelain, earthenware and *bencharong* (five-colour porcelain) into pots, lamp stands and bowls.

For lunch, return to the KM4 post, turn left and drive about 200m (219yds) to **Baan Suan** (tel: 0-5326 2568; daily 11am-8pm), which serves Thai food in a garden setting.

Right: handpainting a giant fan

Northern Thailand

80 km / 50 miles

- ----- Itinerary 12
- ••••• Itinerary 14

12. BALLOON RIDE, ELEPHANT CAMP AND CHIANG DAO CAVES *(see map above)*

Watch sunrise over the Mae Rim Mountains from a hot air balloon. See elephants at work and enjoy a raft trip. If you are feeling fit, make the steep climb into the Chiang Dao Caves.

Oriental Balloon Flights (tel: 0-5339 8609; www.orientalballoonflights.com) runs Thailand's only balloon tours from mid-October to March, subject to weather conditions. Ask to return to your hotel by 9am in time to take up a day tour. There are many elephant camp and rafting tours offered locally; they usually run from 8.30am–3pm, and most visit the Chiang Dao Elephant Training Centre en route to the Chiang Dao Caves.

Rise early for the dawn transfer at around 5am from your hotel to Flora-ville Clubhouse to meet the crew of **Oriental Balloon Flights**. Be sure to dress in layers that you can strip off when the weather gets warmer later. The 90-minute aerial voyage is a superb way of seeing the 'Land of a Million Rice Fields'. To cap the event, a champagne breakfast is served upon landing.

On return to the city join a day tour to see mighty pachyderms at work at the **Chiang Dao Elephant Training Centre** (tel: 0-5329 8553; daily 8am–5pm). The animals play an important part in Thai culture, and for centuries have worked in the teak forests of North Thailand. With logging now outlawed, many are redundant but their deft skills are still displayed for the tourists. After watching them bathe and cavort in the **Ping River**, enjoy a 30-minute elephant trek through the hills.

After lunch at the camp, rafts will take you leisurely down the Ping River. Tours then head up through tobacco plantations to the **Chiang Dao Caves**. Running 1,470m (1,600yds) into the mountains, the caverns are reached by a series of stairs and ladders. The route is quite strenuous: make sure you are reasonably fit. Just beyond the caves is **Wat Tum Pha Plong** (daily 6am–9pm), a picturesque temple.

13. SUKHOTHAI *(see map, p54)*

A visit to the capital of the first independent Thai kingdom, where the remains of more than 20 historical sites and four large lotus ponds can be seen within its old walls.

Sukhothai Historical Park, 427km (266 miles) from Bangkok or 298km (187 miles) from Chiang Mai, is best visited from either of these cities by Bangkok Airways. Alternatively, take an air-conditioned bus or train from either city.

Highway 12 to Old Sukhothai passes through New Sukhothai. About 10km (6 miles) further west, the road reaches the ancient city of **Sukhothai**. The Sukhothai Kingdom (1238–1448) began when King Intradit asserted his independence from the Khmer Empire. Sukhothai, which grew to include most of modern-day Thailand and parts of the Malay Peninsula and Burma, is synonymous with some of the finest artistic achievements in Thai history. The most notable Sukhothai monarch was Ramkhamhaeng (reigned 1280–1318). Among other accomplishments, he reformed the Thai script, promoted Theravada Buddhism and established diplomatic links with China.

The remains of ancient Sukhothai's massive walls reveal that the inner city was protected by three rows of earthen ramparts and two moats. After the Angkorian Empire began to contract, the Khmers departed and the Thais moved in, building their own structures.

Ancient Sites

A short distance from Kamphaenghak Gate is the **Ramkhamhaeng National Museum** (tel: 0-5561 2167; Wed–Sun 9am–4pm; admission fee), a good starting point for a tour of the enclave. The museum contains a fine collection of Sukhothai sculpture, ceramics and other

Above: entrance to Chiang Dao Caves
Right: taking a break

artefacts, as well as exhibits from other periods. The entrance hall is dominated by an impressive bronze image of the walking Buddha. This style of image is regarded as the finest sculptural innovation of the Sukhothai period.

During this period, the Thais invited Theravada Buddhist monks from Sri Lanka to clarify points of scripture. While Buddhism was blossoming, Hindu influence remained strong, indicated by the two bronze images of Hindu gods flanking the walking Buddha in the museum. The first known representation of Thai script, dating from 1292, is displayed on the mezzanine floor – a copy of the famous stone inscription of King Ramkhamhaeng.

Within the walls of Sukhothai are the ruins of some 20 temples and monuments, the greatest of them being **Wat Mahathat** (daily 9am–3pm). It is not known with certainty who founded this shrine, which has been called the 'magical and spiritual centre of the kingdom', but it is presumed to have been the first king of Sukhothai. Wat Mahathat owes its present form to remodelling completed by King Lo Thai, around 1345.

Shrines, Monasteries and Ruins

Next to the museum is **Wat Trapang Thong** (daily 6am–6pm), a small, still functioning temple with fine stucco reliefs. You reach it by crossing the footbridge over the large lotus pond. South of the walled city is another group of shrines and monasteries. One of the most interesting is **Wat Chetupon** (daily 6am–6pm). The walking Buddha here is regarded as one of the finest of its kind.

The elephant, an animal traditionally held in great esteem by the Thais, features prominently at Sukhothai. The 'Elephant Circled Monastery', **Wat Chang Lom** (daily 6am–6pm) about a kilometre east of the main park entrance contains a large bell-shaped stupa supported by 36 elephants sculpted into its base. On another hill west of the city, just south of Wat Saphaan Hin, **Wat Chang Rop** (daily 6am–6pm) also features an elephant-base stupa. **Wat Si Chum** (daily 6am–6pm) to the northwest of the old city wall, has one of the largest seated Buddha images in Thailand. The enclosing shrine (*mondop*) was built in the second half of the 14th century.

About 70km (44 miles) north of Sukhothai, **Si Satchanalai-Chaliang Historical Park** (daily 6am–6pm) is less visited than Sukhothai, but is arguably more attractive. Chaliang dates from the 11th century, and the majority of the ruins at Si Satchanalai date from the 13th to 15th century. The ruins are essentially similar to those at Sukhothai. If this early Thai Kingdom fascinates you, be sure to stop and visit the former kilns at **Sawankhalok**, which are located mid-way between Sukhothai and Si Satchanalai.

Above: Wat Mahathat
Left: set seated Buddha image at Wat Si Chum

14. GOLDEN TRIANGLE *(see map, p54)*

An excursion to Thailand's fabled 'Golden Triangle', including a visit to two of King Mengrai's ancient towns, Chiang Rai and Chiang Saen.

Chiang Rai is 180km (112 miles) from Chiang Mai and accessed by daily bus services (4 hours). Alternatively, travel to Thaton by bus from Chiang Mai, spend the night at a riverside lodge, then follow the Kok River by longtail boat (3–5 hours) to Chiang Rai. The best time for this option is when the river level is high at the end of the rainy season in November.

Chiang Rai is located in Thailand's northernmost province. King Mengrai, who also established Chiang Mai, founded Chiang Rai in the late 1200s. Of interest is the 13th-century **Wat Phra Kaew** on Trairat Road, believed to have been the original residence of the Emerald Buddha that is now found in Bangkok, at the royal temple of the same name. If you have booked a trek to tribal villages in the area, the city's **Hill Tribe Museum** (tel: 0-5371 9167; Mon–Fri 9am–5pm; admission fee) at 620/5 Tanalai Road provides a useful overview of tribal community life.

The town makes a convenient base for exploring further into the Golden Triangle. From Chiang Rai, follow H110 north to Mae Chan. Slightly north of the town the road splits: take H1016 to the right and continue for about 20km (12½ miles) to the ancient capital of Chiang Saen.

Golden Triangle

Chiang Saen is located near where Burma, Laos and Thailand meet. This area, known as the **Golden Triangle**, has for years produced almost half of the world's opium supply. Thailand's contribution has dropped significantly in the past decade, but Burma and Laos continue to grow the opium poppy. Chiang Saen was founded around the end of the 13th century. The town's lovely setting on the Mekong River strongly enhances the charm of its old temples.

Head north for around 9km (5½ miles) and you will come to the small town of **Sop Ruak**, the heart of the Golden Triangle. Its main street is lined with textile and souvenirs shops, food stalls and restaurants. The **Opium Exhibition Hall** (Moo 1; tel: 0-5378 4444; Tue–Sun 10am–3.30pm; admission fee), which cost US$10 million to build, has cleverly designed galleries and multimedia exhibits covering 300 years of opium history in Asia. Just opposite the museum is the **Anantara Resort and Spa** (tel: 0-5378 4084; www.anantara.com), which has a working elephant camp and a spa on site.

Continuing northwest out of Sop Ruak, the road reaches **Mae Sai**, the most northerly town in Thailand. With the town of Tachilek in Burma (Myanmar) clearly visible across the small Sai River, this border town has a real frontier feel. In the shops along the main streets Burmese, Thai, Shan and hill tribe traders sell gems, lacquerware, antiques and medicinal herbs.

Right: Chiang Rai city pillars

15. MAE HONG SON *(see map, p54)*

Shan-style temples and a valley setting make Mae Hong Son, located close to the Burmese border, one of the North's most beautiful towns.

Mae Hong Son, 125 km (78 miles) northwest of Chiang Mai, is best reached by a THAI flight (see page 93) from Chiang Mai. Buses make the same journey but take between 8–9 hours. This area is most beautiful during the cool season from November to March. Nights can be cold so bring some warm clothes.

Mae Hong Son lies in a valley between forested mountains, which accounts for its early morning fogs. For years, it has been a destination for seekers of peace and tranquillity, notwithstanding the fact that it is smack in the middle of an area known for border smuggling activities. Adding colour to the area are Karen, Lisu, Hmong, Shan and other hill tribes, who easily outnumber the ethnic Thais.

On arrival, check in at your hotel, then spend some time absorbing the atmosphere at **Jong Kum Lake** and its two temples, **Wat Jong Klang** and **Wat Jong Kum**. Both are fine examples of Burmese architecture, with their tiny roofs stacked one atop the other and the filigree fretwork along their eaves. The gilded stupa is a prime example of Burmese design with its terraced base, squat body and spire of discs rising to a crown.

In the afternoon, walk to **Wat Phra Non** and its 12-m (39-ft)-long **reclining Buddha** statue, depicting him at death. Cross the road and ascend a steep stairway to **Wat Phra That Doi Kong Mu**. Erected in the 19th century reflecting Burmese influences, the temple comprises two beautiful stupa and a superb view of the valley. From the parapet, watch the sun set over the town.

Fern Restaurant (tel: 0-5361 1374) on Khunlumprapat Road serves excellent local dishes for dinner. The restaurant looks out over the lake and is on the same street as the busy **Night Market**. Look for handicraft stores along **Singhanat Bamrung Road** or check out the city centre department store called **Kad Kam** (tel: 0-5362 0161, daily 7am–9pm).

Above: Wat Phra That Doi Kong Mu

Northeast
Thailand

The poorest area of Thailand, the Northeast, is seldom visited by tourists, though it is home to one-third of Thailand's population. Its language and culture are similar to those of Laos; indeed, other Thais often refer to Northeastern, or Isaan, people as 'Lao'. Five hundred years ago, the Lao Kingdom of Lan Xang, or 'One Million Elephants', spanned a broad swathe of mainland Southeast Asia, stretching from Vietnam in the east to Burma in the west, whilst encompassing much of present-day North and Northeast Thailand. In the following centuries the Lao fell on hard times. Caught between the Vietnamese hammer and the Siamese anvil, the once powerful Kingdom of a Million Elephants was reduced to a shadow of its former self, forced to pay tribute to both Hue and Bangkok, becoming – in the derisory Siamese idiom of the time – 'a bird with two heads'. This division was enshrined with the advent of French imperialism in the late 19th century, when the former Lao Kingdom was permanently divided into two parts. Today, Laos and Northeast Thailand, or Isaan, are sundered by the waters of the Mekong River.

There are three principal reasons why, in recent years, more tourists have been heading towards the Northeast. Firstly, increased ease of access to Laos means that with a visa, one can cross the border at Nong Khai in the North, at Mukdahan in the East and at Chong Mek in the South. Secondly, people want to see the remains of Khmer temples constructed by the rulers of the great Angkor Empire in the 11th and 12th centuries. Finally, there are those who like the Northeast because of its unaffected, informal people and the traditional Thai way of life that is perpetuated here. Once known for its poverty, standards of living in Isaan have now improved markedly. Numerous projects to improve agricultural production, processing and transport have been fairly successful.

Itineraries 17 and *18* might alternatively be called the 'Khmer Culture Trail', a concept that has been heartily embraced by the PR people at the Tourism Authority of Thailand (TAT). Khorat, officially known as Nakhon Ratchasima, is the largest town in the Northeast and should be regarded as your base from which to start *Itinerary 16*. Khao Phra Viharn *(Itinerary 17)*, one of the most impressive Khmer sites, is found in Cambodia. You won't need a visa but you must remember to bring along your passport. It's best visited in a day from the large Northeastern city of Ubon Ratchathani.

Right: an Isaan woman

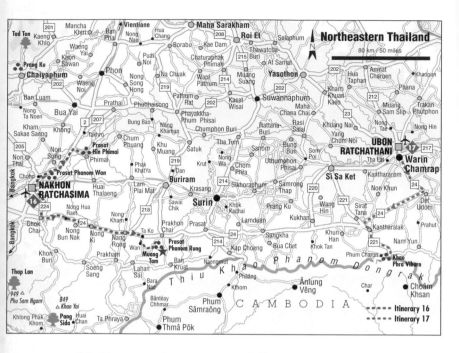

16. NAKHON RATCHASIMA & ENVIRONS *(see map above)*

Take a two-day trip to Nakhon Ratchasima (Khorat) to visit the Prasat Phanom Wan sanctuary, the ruins of Phimai, and the impressively restored Khmer hilltop temple, Prasat Phanom Rung.

Located 250km (155 miles) from Bangkok, Nakhon Ratchasima can be accessed from Bangkok by buses (4 hours), which leave from Bangkok's Northern Bus Terminal, and or by trains (5 hours) from Hualamphong Station. Once in Nakhon Ratchasima, arrange for a private car with a driver.

Most of Nakhon Ratchasima's attractions lie outside the city. Two of the sites, Prasat Phanom Wan and Prasat Hin Phimai (known simply as 'Phimai'), lie within close reach of the city. Hire a hotel taxi for the day and drive out 14km (9 miles) north on H2. Turn right onto a dirt road that, 4km (2½ miles) later, reaches the remote sanctuary of **Prasat Phanom Wan** (tel: 0-4447 1167, daily 8am–6pm; admission fee).

　These 11th-century sandstone ruins have corbelled roofs, delicately carved lintels, spires and false windows with stone mullions that echo the grandeur of Angkor Wat. Unlike most Khmer ruins in the Northeast, the central sanctuary is still used for worship. Behind its vaulted entrance are recent Buddha images of different styles, most of them covered with gold leaf.

The Ruins of Phimai

To reach Phimai, continue north on H2 for another 20km (12½ miles), then right for 10km (6 miles) to the ruins of **Prasat Hin Phimai**, one of Thailand's best-preserved Khmer ruins. Built by the last of the great Angkorian

Top right: carved lintel, Prasat Phanom Rung
Right: entrance to Prasat Hin Phimai

monarchs, King Jayavarman VII (1181–1201), its original entrance gate still stands at the end of Phimai's present main street. Wander through its sanctuaries, noticing the lintels and pausing to contemplate the marvellous sense of perspective the architects achieved. Near the Mun River Bridge is a museum displaying some of Phimai's superbly carved lintels and statues.

Many visitors spend a night in **Phimai**, a pleasant town on the Mun River. The unpretentious **Old Phimai Guesthouse** along Chonsudaset Road (tel: 0-4447 1918) is ideal as it is located close to the temple ruins. If you stay, ask the locals for directions to the country's oldest and largest banyan tree on Route 206. **Sai Ngam** (Beautiful Banyan), 1km (½ mile) east of the temple, has a dense canopy that locals believe shelters spirits.

Prasat Phanom Rung

Return to Nakhon Ratchasima for lunch, then drive south on H224 to Chok Chai and east on H24. After 80km (50 miles) the road forks; take the right fork and proceed another 18km (11 miles) to Ban Ta Ko. Turn right at the sign for **Prasat Phanom Rung** (daily 9am–4pm). Follow the road to Ban Wan and bear left to reach this Khmer hilltop temple that historians believe was an important outpost between Angkor and Phimai during the 11th and 12th centuries.

The Khmers were masters in marrying site to architecture. They liked long, sweeping staircases and esplanades to convey grandeur. Running along the spine of the hill and interrupted by landings, the monumental stairway exudes the mass and power typical of Khmer design. At the summit is the restored sanctuary whose main *prang* (spire), galleries and chapels reflect the geometric precision of Angkorian architecture with symmetrical doors and windows, and antechapels facing the four cardinal points. Enjoy the view.

17. CAMBODIA'S PRASAT KHAO PHRA VIHARN
(see maps, p60 and below)

An arduous climb to the magnificent cliff-top Khmer temple complex of Prasat Khao Phra Viharn, situated in Cambodia but, ironically, more easily accessed across the border from Thailand.

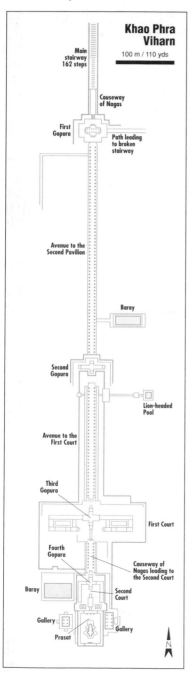

There are slow trains and overnight buses that cover the 557-km (346-mile) distance between Bangkok and Ubon Ratchathani, the jumping-off point for Prasat Khao Phra Viharn. However, most people fly from Bangkok on THAI. The flight takes only a little over an hour. There are also bus services between Nakhon Ratchasima and Ubon Ratchathani. From Ubon Ratchathani, arrange for a car and driver to take you Phum Charon, the closest point in Thailand to the temple. Remember to take your passport as you will cross the border into Cambodia.

A Khmer architectural masterpiece, **Prasat Khao Phra Viharn** (tel: 0-4561 9214; daily 7.30am–4.30pm; admission fee) is set high on a cliff on the edge of the Dongrak Mountains overlooking Cambodia. By an anomaly of history, Prasat Khao Phra Viharn officially belongs to Cambodia but can only be reached from Ubon Ratchathani province in Thailand.

In the early 1960s, the World Court awarded the temple to Cambodia. Known as Preah Vihear by the Cambodians, it was closed for decades because of civil war. It opened briefly between 1991 and 1993, only to become off-limits again due to the presence of Khmer Rouge forces in the region. In August 1998, following the death of Pol Pot and the expulsion of the Khmer Rouge from their nearby base at Anglong Veng in Cambodia, the temple opened once more and has remained so, apart from a brief spell in early 2003. Check with Bangkok's TAT office before embarking on this long trip.

Temple History
Construction work on this nearly 1-km (½-mile) long temple began during the reign of Rajendravarman II in the mid-10th cen-

tury and reached completion during the reign of Surayavarman II in the early 12th century. It was the latter monarch, truly a visionary builder, who also began the construction of Angkor Wat. It is thought that, for at least 500 years before the building of Prasat Khao Phra Viharn, the site was considered holy by the Khmers.

Although in need of restoration, Prasat Khao Phra Viharn is an extraordinary place, possibly the most impressive Khmer historical site after Angkor. One is left wondering how the original builders transported the massive blocks of stone to the peak of the Dongrak escarpment, a height of 600m (1,968ft). At the summit is a stupendous view of the Cambodian plain below.

A Pilgrimage Site

Prasat Khao Phra Viharn was built originally as a Hindu temple dedicated to the god Shiva. Constructed in the Baphuon and early Angkor styles, the complex comprises a series of long stairways ascending from ridge to ridge, and on each landing, the shells of Hindu temples, used later by Buddhists after Khmer monarchs converted in the 12th century.

Of the four principal *gopura*, or elaborately decorated gateways, the first two are in a serious state of disrepair, though some fine examples of carving – *apsaras* (celestial dancers) and various divinities – can still be distinguished upon them. The third *gopura* is comparatively well preserved, with a delicately carved lintel that depicts Shiva and his consort Uma sitting on Nandi, the bull.

Foreign (ie, non-Thai) visitors to Prasat Khao Phra Viharn must pay a 200 baht entry fee per head and deposit their passports with the Thai border police. The new black-top road to the temple stops abruptly at the Thai frontier, and visitors then proceed on foot across a rocky plateau, down a steep embankment, and up a long slope to the initial – steep and tricky – temple steps. It's not a climb for the old or unfit, though many elderly Thai pilgrims, tiny old ladies prominent amongst them, pull themselves to the top of the hill.

The temple extends for around 900m (2,952ft), through five separate stages, before culminating in the massive bulk of the main sanctuary perched high on the cliff top. Here the great *prasat* or central spire has been thrown to the ground and mighty blocks of carved stone lie in a tumbled heap, awaiting eventual restoration. Everywhere, there are signs warning visitors not to stray off the sanctioned paths, because the danger from land mines remains very real.

Above: lower entrance, Prasat Khao Phra Viharn

South Thailand

S outhern Thailand is where Thai-speaking Buddhists live together with Muslims of Malay origin. It is a land of verdant jungles and limestone peaks, azure seas and spicy coconut-flavoured dishes. The region is crisscrossed by a network of excellent roads which connect the Andaman Coast with the Gulf of Thailand all the way to Hat Yai and the Malaysian frontier.

The twin Andaman Sea and Gulf of Thailand coastlines offer pristine beaches and islands, friendly, predominantly rural communities, and markets overflowing with exotic fruits and other native produce. It's a land of plenty, where travellers can revel by the beach, or explore the ancient sites of the Srivijayan kingdom.

As a whole, the region is very peaceful and safe, but the three southeasternmost provinces – Yala, Pattani and Narathiwat – have endured politically motivated violence at the hands of Thai Muslim nationalists who want the three provinces to become part of an independent Muslim state that would also include two states of neighbouring Malaysia. Travel to this area is hence best avoided.

The tsunami of December 2004 wrecked destruction on an unprecedented scale along South Thailand's Andaman coast and claimed over 8,000 lives. However, international and local relief and reconstruction efforts saw most places along the coast returning to normal within six months of the tragedy. Ko Phi Phi Don took a little longer to recover, and today, only Bang Niang beach in Khao Lak, which took the greatest hit from the tsunami, still suffers from the after-effects of the world's most talked-about natural disaster.

From a small island known only to tin miners, rubber planters and fishermen two decades ago, Phuket (*Itinerary 18*) has blossomed into Asia's premier beach resort. Its appeal lies in its stunning powder soft beaches, balmy weather and wealth of activities as well as excellent eating options. Yet despite its rapid development, there are still corners of the island that offer pristine forests, waterfalls and good walking trails; and not all beaches are full of jet-skiing holidaymakers.

Phuket Town is the main hub from which travellers venture out to the quieter islands. Measuring only 587sq km (226sq miles), Phuket can be explored by jeep or slightly more unusual forms of transport: bike, elephant or kayak. Brightly painted buses ply regular routes between the main towns and beaches.

Lesser known but equally attractive are Phuket's provincial neighbours: Phang Nga (*Itinerary 19*) and Krabi (*Itinerary 20*). The lush green forests of this region and the multitude of nearby small islands, such as Ko Phi Phi (*Itinerary 21*), offer spectacular scenery and some of the best reef diving in the world. Another hotspot is Ko Samui (*Itinerary 22*), the South's second-largest island and now bursting with 5-star hotels, trendy spas and new restaurants.

Left: idyllic Ko Phi Phi
Right: the good life

18. PHUKET *(see map, p67)*

A multitude of white sandy beaches to satisfy any aficionado as well as several green pockets of superb beauty that are well worth exploring.

Phuket is easily reached from Bangkok by flight (THAI, Orient Thai and AirAsia; see page 93). For this itinerary, hire a car to explore Phuket's varied beaches. The best place to do so is at one of the many car hire desks at the airport or Patong beach along the west coast.

Phuket's beaches share the same powdery sand, blue-green water, and casuarina and palm trees, yet each is unique. The best beaches line the western shore of the island. The following are the key beaches, running from north to south. With 9km (5½ miles) of snowy white sand, **Mai Khao** (White Wood), north of the airport, is Phuket's longest beach. The northern mangrove area and the former Nai Yang National Park further south are now preserved as the **Sirinat National Park**. As a result, construction here has been controlled; there are only a few small thatched restaurants and only one major resort, the eco-friendly **JW Marriott Resort & Spa** (tel: 0-7633 8000; www.marriott.com).

Northerly Beaches

To reach **Nai Yang** beach from Mai Khao, return to the town of Suan Maphrao and take Thep Kra Satri Road (H402) towards the airport for 10km (6½ miles). Turn right into H4026 and follow the signs for **Indigo Pearl** (tel: 0-7632 7006; www.indigo-pearl.com), the only resort of note in this area. The Olive Ridley sea turtles are the main reason for the beach's protected status. Between November and February, Mai Khao and Nai Yang beaches play host to hundreds of these shy creatures, which come ashore in the evenings to lay their eggs. The Sirinat National Park Visitors' Centre (tel: 0-7632 7407) maintains several bungalows, which can be rented for 200–800 baht a night.

Leaving Nai Yang on the H4026, continue south to the pretty village of

Above: beach bums at Phuket

Ban Sakhu. On entering the village, take the small road to the right and follow the signs for 4km (2½ miles) to the quiet **Nai Thon** beach. There are a number of small restaurants serving grilled seafood. Opposite, the **Phuket Naithon Resort** (tel: 0-7620 5233; www.phuketnaithonresort.com) offers comfortable mid- to upper-range bungalows. To the south, perched on a hill overlooking beautiful **Hin Kruai Bay**, is the **Trisara** (tel: 0-7631 0100; www.trisara.com), one of the island's most exclusive hideaways.

The coastal road continues south to **Bang Thao** beach. Although the beach is dominated by the luxurious **Laguna Phuket** multi-resort development (www.lagunaphuket.com), it is possible to find a quiet corner to swim in. From Bang Thao, the road skirts the various lagoons until it joins the H4025 just beyond Choeng Thale, where the **Hideaway Day Spa** (tel: 0-7634 0591; www.phuket-hideaway.com) is located.

Turning right, head towards the Muslim village of Bang Thao and on to the next two beaches 3km (1½ miles) away. **Pansea** beach has a beautiful cove anchored by huge boulders. One of the best beaches on the island, it is shared by two upmarket resorts, **The Chedi Phuket** (tel: 0-7632 4017; www.ghm hotels.com) and **Amanpuri** (tel: 0-7632 4333; www.amanpuri.com).

Surin beach is also as yet undeveloped – and for good reason: from May to November the water can have a dangerous undertow. If you enjoy seafood, try one of the small restaurants at the southern end. Continuing south along the coast road is **Kamala** beach, which has less undertow. There are small, low-budget bungalows at the northern end. The fishing village located next to the beach is a good place to sample southern Thailand's Muslim cuisine.

Central Coast Beaches

About 8km (5 miles) further south on the coastal road you will find Phuket's busiest beach resort. **Patong**, a 4-km (2½-mile)-long crescent beach 15km (9½ miles) west of Phuket Town, is the most developed of Phuket's beaches. Here you will find Phuket's largest hotels and the widest array of watersports facilities, shops, bars and restaurants. Patong beach was hard hit by the tsunami in December 2004, but it has recovered completely. From Patong, visitors can take a 45-minute longtail boat ride to **Freedom Beach**, located just around the headland.

Moving south from Patong, you'll eventually reach **Relax Bay**. Sometimes referred to as Karon Noi, it contains a single hotel, **Le Meridien Phuket** (tel: 0-76 37 0100; www.lemeridien.com).

Just over Laem Khak lies **Karon** beach. At more than 4km (2½ miles) in length, it is one of Phuket's longest beaches. The towns of Ban Karon and Ban Kata blend into each other these

Phuket map

days, such has been the speed of development. **Kata Yai**, south of Karon, is a spectacularly beautiful beach. If you are a reasonably strong swimmer, the small offshore island of **Ko Pu**, is worth a swim. Relatively shallow waters make it one of the best beaches on the island for snorkelling. **Club Med** (tel: 0-7633 0455; www.clubmed.co.th) and the **Mom Tri's Boathouse** (tel: 0-7633 0015; www.boathousephuket.com) provide the best accommodation here. The expensive **Villa Royale** (tel: 0-7633 3569; www.villaroyalephuket.com),

with its six luxurious Thai-style villas, is perched on the cliff and overlooks the adjacent bay, Kata Noi. This idyllic and beautiful white-sand beach is fronted by the 4-star **Katathani Resort** (tel: 0-7633 0124; www.katathani.com). There is some decent snorkelling at both ends of the bay, and surfing at the north end when conditions are right.

The South and Interior

To reach the southernmost parts of Phuket, retrace your steps up the hill from Kata Noi, and at the top, turn right and follow the signs to the 'Viewpoint'. From here, you'll have a splendid view of Karon, Kata Yai and Kata Noi beaches. The road then swings inland, running through rubber plantations and picturesque rice paddies.

Eventually after some 4km (2½ miles) you will reach another lovely beach on the island, **Nai Harn**. It lies between two ridges and faces the setting sun. Behind it is the beautiful lagoon that gives it its name. Offshore is the island of Ko Kaew Yai. Situated at the northern end of the beach is one of the island's premier hotels, **Le Royal Meridien Phuket Yacht Club** (tel: 0-7638 0200; www.lemeridien.com). This beach is also the site of the Phuket King's Cup Regatta in December each year.

From Nai Harn, follow the road (H4233) around the scenic Promthep headland and on to Phuket's southernmost tip, **Rawai** beach. At the eastern end of the beach are some small seafood restaurants. The main hotel on Rawai is the stylish **Evason Phuket** resort (tel: 0-7638 1010; www.evasonresorts.com) with its excellent in-house spa. Just offshore is a private island where the Evason's guests while away their time.

When you are tired of sand and sea, set off for the interior. Drive on H402 (the airport road) north to the old capital city of Thalang. At the traffic lights, turn right and drive down a shady 4-km (2½-mile) corridor of rubber trees to the Forestry Department checkpoint. The fork on the left takes you into **Khao Phra Thaew National Park** (daily 6am–6pm). Park and walk the 250-m (273-yd) trail to **Ton Sai Waterfall**, taking the middle path. In the dry season, the waterfall is barely a trickle but in the monsoon season, it becomes a torrent.

Returning to the car park, drive back towards Thalang. On reaching Thalang, turn right onto H402 and drive north for about 1km (½ mile). About 500m (547yds) down the side road is **Wat Phra Thong**, or 'Temple of the

Above: Rawai fishing boats
Right: exploring a cave at Phang Nga

Golden Buddha Image', the second-most important Buddhist temple on the island. Its fame lies in the half-buried Buddha image in the ordination hall, though it is not the most aesthetically pleasing of images. Standing at 2m (7ft) tall, it is exposed from the middle of the chest up. It appears to be in a seated position, suggesting that a full height of about 4m (13ft). The incense smoke in the room helps evoke an ethereal atmosphere. According to legend, anyone who tries to unearth the statue will meet with a grisly death.

19. PHANG NGA BAY *(see map, p71)*

A day-long boat trip past mysterious monoliths and some of Asia's most spectacular scenery. Alternatively take a canoe into some of the beautiful sea caves and lagoons in the bay.

Most Phuket tour companies will pick you up from your hotel at about 8am for the 70–90 minute drive to the bay. From the Phang Nga Bay Resort jetty, you travel by longtail boat past islands shaped like beasts.

The islands in Phang Nga Bay, 75km (46½ miles) northeast of Phuket, are among the wonders of Asia, rivalling and perhaps even surpassing Vietnam's famed Halong Bay. Together, the islands make up **Ao Phang Nga National Park**, which covers an area of about 400sq km (154sq miles). Sheer-sided limestone monoliths rise 300m (980ft) out of the sea like the ethereal mountains in Chinese paintings, particularly breathtaking in the early morning light.

The first stop is **Ko Ping Kan**, also known as 'James Bond Island' as it was featured in the Bond film, *The Man With the Golden Gun*. The waters in front of Ko Ping Kan hold a geological oddity called **Ko Tapu** (Nail Island). Rising from a precariously thin base 200m (650ft) out of the water, like the Leaning Tower of Pisa, the island seems destined to tip into the water at some future date.

The boat then moves on to **Ko Panyi**, an island with a Muslim village built entirely on stilts next to a limestone mountain, and housing some 500 families. There's an attractive, green-roofed mosque sheltering in the lee of the great cliff, which dominates the village. Don't hesitate to go in – providing, of course, you are properly clad and it is not during prayers. As is the case elsewhere in Thailand, Islam is decidedly laid-back here.

The return boat journey is generally via **Tham Lawd**, a natural tunnel that runs beneath a huge mountain. It then stops at **Khao Khian** for passengers to see drawings of ancient ships on its rock walls, visible only from the water. Many tours also visit **Tham Suwan Ku Ha**, a limestone cave 12km (7½ miles) from Phang Nga. The caves hold Buddha images illuminated by a shaft of sunlight pouring through a hole in the ceiling. This cave is well worth the trip, so ask if it is included in your tour.

Sea Canoe Option

It's possible to take day trips or multi-day excursions by sea canoe in the Phang Nga Bay area. Sea-canoeing is an eco-friendly way to explore the wonders of the bay. Holding two passengers and a paddler, the canoes are manoeuvred into caves and tunnels under huge limestone mountains rising from the bay.

Many of these monoliths are doughnut-shaped, hollow in the centre and open to the sky. The paddler times his entry to coincide with ebbing tides, and squeezes through narrow passages. You emerge into a silent lagoon with mangroves and cliff-clinging trees inhabited by kingfishers and wildlife stranded there when the seas rose eons ago. For details, contact **Sea Canoe Thailand** (tel: 0-7621 2172; www.seacanoe.net) at 367/4 Yaowaraj Road, Phuket Town. There are also offices in Ko Samui and Krabi.

20. KRABI *(see map, p71)*

Located on the mainland to the east of Phuket, Krabi province comprises more than 5,000sq km (1,930sq miles) of jungled hills together with a gorgeous Andaman Sea coastline and around 200 islands.

Travel to Krabi from Bangkok by air-conditioned coach (12 hours) or by flights operated by several airlines (THAI, Orient Thai and AirAsia; see page 93). From Phuket, it's a 2½–3-hour drive through Phang-nga province. THAI also flies between Phuket and Krabi.

Krabi province has four main areas of interest: the town, beaches, islands and the interior. **Krabi** town, 815km (507 miles) from Bangkok, is located on the Krabi River with its extensive mangrove forests on the opposite bank.

Above: Ko Tapu

You could hire a longtail boat for bird watching in the mangrove canals or visit the **Khao Kanab Nam** limestone twin peaks and its huge cave. Good accommodation is available at the Viengthong, Thai and Meritime hotels. In the evenings, you can dine out at one of the two simple night markets. Krabi's beaches, notably, Ao Nang, Nopparat Thara, Railay and Phra Nang, are some distance from town but all are easily accessed by road and by boat.

World-class Beaches

Ao Nang beach, 15km (9 miles) by bus from town, is the most popular, and also the most developed. The water is clean, but the beach is often crowded with longtail boats, whose piercing engine noise is annoying. Ao Nang is also the longest of Krabi's beaches, with a wide range of restaurants and accommodation to suit all budgets. Many people stay in Ao Nang and take a longtail boat to Railay and Hat Tham Phra Nang beaches 3km (2 miles) away on the cape of Laem Phra Nang. Acclaimed as being among the most attractive in the world, they have fine sands flanked by 200-m (650-ft)-tall limestone outcrops.

Railay beach is actually divided into **Railay East** and **Railay West** beaches. The former is rather muddy at low tide and the latter is sandier and generally more attractive.

In between the two Railay beaches is **Hat Tham Phra Nang** beach, beyond question the most beautiful

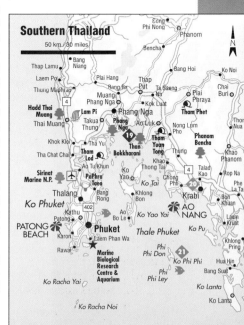

Above: chicken-shaped island near Krabi

beach in the Krabi region and one of the loveliest in Thailand. Named after a mythical princess called Phra Nang, the beach is made up of fine, soft and clean sand backed by tall limestone cliffs. If you visit the cave of **Tham Phra Nang**, set in the limestone cliffs, you will see that it is well-stocked with wooden phalluses. These are placed there as offerings to the princess by the local fishermen – in the hope of ensuring good harvests. On the headland of Phra Nang beach is the luxurious **Rayavadee Resort** (tel: 0-7562 0740; www.rayavadee.com) with its unobtrusive Thai-style pavilions.

Also worth a visit is the **Noppharat Thara** beach, just 3km (2 miles) northwest of Ao Nang. The name – which means 'Beach of the Nine-Jewelled Stream' – is derived from a small waterway that flows into the Andaman Sea at this point. The beach is around 2km (1¼ miles) long and forms part of the Hat Noppharat Thara – Ko Phi Phi National Park *(Itinerary 21)*, which provides the area with a degree of protection against environmental damage. There are a few small hotels, restaurants and bars along this beach.

East of Noppharat Thara is **Khlong Muang** beach, which has a nice ambience and hosts the luxurious **Sheraton Krabi** (tel: 0-7562 8000; www.sheraton.com/krabi) and the boutique resort **Nakamanda** (tel: 0-7564 4388; www.nakamanda.com).

If based in Krabi, visit the **Khao Phanom Bencha National Park**, north of Krabi Town, which rises to 1,350m (4,430ft) and is clad in dense primary forest. This 500-sq km (190-sq mile) park is home to more than 30 mammal species, including the Asiatic black bear, the Malaysian sun bear and the rare clouded leopard, plus nearly 200 species of birds.

Just 9km (6 miles) from Krabi Town is **Wat Tham Seua**, the 'Tiger Cave Temple' (daily 8am–6pm; admission fee). At its rear is a concrete staircase; clambering the 1,272 steps up the 600-metre (1,970-ft) peak brings you to a small shrine and a footprint of the Buddha immortalised in a flat rock.

Islands Near Krabi

There are lots of interesting boat tours you can book from the Krabi resorts that visit stunning outlying islands like **Ko Poda**, 6km (4 miles) from Ao

Nang. Poda comprises two tiny islets linked by a strip of sand that disappears at high tide. **Ko Hong** is a stunning turquoise lagoon seemingly 'walled' in by huge cliffs.

Ko Lanta, an unspoilt island to the south of the province that is part of a national marine park, is rapidly growing in popularity as an alternative to Krabi. It is reached by a combination of car and boat from Krabi Town. The once exclusively budget accommodations scattered down the west coast from the main town of **Ban Sala Dan** are now joined by luxury resorts like the **Pimalai Resort & Spa** (tel: 0-7560 7999; www.pimalai.com), **Sri Lanta** (tel: 0-7566 2688; www.srilanta.com) and a boutique resort, **Costa Lanta** (tel: 0-7568 4630; www.costalanta.com).

Left: gorgeous Hat Tham Phra Nang beach

21. KO PHI PHI *(see map, p71)*

Set in the centre of the Sea of Phuket, Phi Phi consists of two islands, Phi Phi Don and Phi Phi Ley. Take a boat to these jewel-like islands from either Krabi or Phuket, with the option of staying overnight or longer.

Phi Phi is almost equidistant from Phuket and Krabi and can be reached from either place in around 2 hours by boat. Services are subject to weather conditions and rarely operate during the monsoon.

Phi Phi Don and **Phi Phi Ley**, the twin islands collectively known as **Ko Phi Phi** (pronounced 'Pee Pee') are two of the most stunning islands in Asia. They sit at the southern end of the Phang Nga chain, 34km (21 miles) from Phuket and about 40km (25 miles) from Krabi. The larger of the two, Phi Phi Don, 20km (12½ miles) in circumference, comprises two enormous mountains linked by a very narrow strip of sand. Nine coves of powdery sand, adjoining coral reefs and warm aquamarine waters give the island its reputation for unsurpassed beauty.

Phi Phi Don's Beaches

Two back-to-back bays, **Lo Dalam** and **Ton Sai**, separated by a narrow sand isthmus, are the focus of most development on the island. The tsunami in 2004 damaged both beaches very heavily, with many beachfront establishments totally destroyed. Most places have been rebuilt, and today, there is very sign of the havoc caused by the colossal tsunami.

A large flat rock located high on a bluff at the southern end of the island at **Lo Dalum** offers grand vistas of island and sea. To get there, walk over the rocky headland at the south end of Ton Sai beach. Just past the bridge is an arrow to the left. Follow it and walk 45 minutes up a steep hill. At the top you'll see the twin bays of Phi Phi Don barely separated by a thin strip of land.

The southern beaches, the most popular of which is **Hat Yao**, have more

Above: Phi Phi Don's twin bays

rudimentary bungalows designed for budget travellers. The more luxurious resorts are on the east-facing beaches, **Laem Thong** and **Lo Bakao**: **Phi Phi Island Village** (tel: 0-7621 5014; www.ppisland.com), **Zeavola Resort** (tel: 0-7562 7000; www.zeavola.com) and **Holiday Inn Resort** (tel: 0-7562 1334; www.phiphi-palmbeach.com).

The smaller Phi Phi Ley lies about 4km (2½ miles) south of Phi Phi Don. It attracts thousands of swifts that build nests prized by Chinese gourmets for birds' nest soup. Swarms descend on Phi Phi Ley between January and April to spend about two weeks in the caves building nests held together by their saliva. A popular trip is to the **Viking Cave**, whose walls are decorated with a mixture of prehistoric murals representing human and animal forms, together with more recent, probably 19th-century, representations of Chinese junks. **Maya Bay**, on its western shore, has been hailed as one of the most beautiful bays in the world and in 1999 played host to the filming of *The Beach*. It is however overrun with visitors.

22. KO SAMUI *(see map, p75)*

The paradisiacal island of Ko Samui, first developed as a budget traveller's paradise in the 1970s, has since moved considerably upmarket.

Ko Samui can be reached by ferry from Surat Thani or by air from Bangkok or Phuket. There are regular ferry services from Ko Samui to outlying islands such as Ko Phangan and Ko Tao.

In the last few years, Thailand's third-largest island, at 250sq km (97sq miles), has been transformed from a sleepy backwater to a mainstream resort island with a plethora of late-night shopping malls, New Age healing retreats, luxury hotels and an 18-hole golf course. A new highway

circles the whole island, linking all the main towns. The island's idyllic beaches, hills, waterfalls and rocky coves support a thriving economy based on tourism and coconut cultivation, with fishing a third mainstay.

A selection of landscaped resorts and a vibrant nightlife scene are centred around **Chaweng** beach, on the island's east side. Chaweng has the largest choice of mostly mid-range accommodations. Gently curving bays with fine white sand and crystal-clear waters follow each other in succession over a distance of 6km (3½ miles). The popular **Samui Institute of Thai Culinary Arts** (tel: 0-7741 3172; www.sitca.net) is also in Chaweng, offering morning and afternoon cooking classes in English from Monday to Saturday.

South of Chaweng is **Lamai** beach, with its small plots of family-owned land. At the centre, almost directly on the beach, is an entertainment strip filled with discos, pubs and a few bars.

On the western side of the island, the main port and largest town, **Na Thon**, has a distinctive Chinese mercantile character, evident in the wooden shop houses along Angthong Lane. Ferries to Ko Phangan and Ang Thong National Marine Park depart from here.

For more panorama, head along the north shore to **Maenam**. The sand is coarser than in the east, but the 4-km (2½-mile) stretch is little developed and accommodation is cheaper, with the exception of the upscale **Santiburi Resort** (tel: 0-7 742 5031; www.santiburi.com). Almost the entire northern coast of Ko Samui is made up of lovely secluded bays. The next bay to the east is **Bo Phut**, the only beach on the island where tourists and islanders live side by side, and where a certain amount of local lifestyle can be observed. On a cliff further east sits the island's major landmark, a huge Buddha statue. **Bangrak** beach, which ends by the cliff, is also known as **Big Buddha beach**. On the island's northeastern spur is the quieter **Choeng Mon**.

Ko Phangan and a Marine Park

Just 12km (7½ miles) north of Samui is **Ko Phangan**, a smaller island with the same inviting topography and fine sandy beaches, mostly popular with Western budget travellers living in simple beach huts around the island's coast. Ko Phangan is good territory to explore by mountain bike, available for hire in its only town, **Tong Sala**. Most travellers go to **Had Rin** beach on the island's southeastern tip, where the uninhibited full-moon beach parties attended by thousands have acquired a certain notoriety.

The **Ang Thong National Marine Park,** 30km (19 miles) west of Samui, is a popular destination for a day trip. The main attractions here include some superlative snorkelling, an exhilarating hike up to the 400-m (1,300-ft)-high viewpoint, which has a panoramic view over the 40 uninhabited islands, and a swim in a 5-ha (12-acre) inland lake.

Left top: Ton Sai beach, Phi Phi Don
Left: Chaweng beach, Ko Samui

Leisure Activities

shopping

SHOPPING

Thailand is a huge emporium of art and craft products. While each region has its own specialities, goods from all regions are available in Bangkok, Chiang Mai and Phuket. You find the widest selection of goods and the best prices in Bangkok and Chiang Mai. Pay street vendors in cash; large shops will accept credit cards but expect to pay a 3–5 percent surcharge. Shops can arrange packing and shipping at reasonable rates.

Antiques: There are wood, bronze, terracotta and stone statues from all regions, plus carved wooden angels, mythical animals and temple bargeboards. The Thai government prohibits the export of Buddha images, but images of other deities and disciples can be sent abroad. Genuine antiques are in increasingly short supply, and Thailand's artisans now create copies (no attempt is made to sell them as antiques) and the craftsmanship is quite remarkable.

Baskets: Thailand's abundant wicker and grasses are transformed into lampshades, storage boxes, colourful mats, handbags, letter holders, tissue boxes and slippers. Wicker and bamboo are turned into storage lockers and furniture. *Yan lipao*, a sturdy grass about the thickness of a broom straw, is woven into delicately patterned purses and bags.

Ceramics: Most Thai ceramic items come from the North. Best known is celadon, the jade-green, brown, or cobalt statues, lamps and other items distinguished by finely glazed surfaces. There are also blue-and-white porcelain pots, lamp bases, household items and figurines, and earthenware pots, planters and dinner sets in a rainbow of hues. Also popular are the brown-glazed jars bearing *dom* or dragon designs which are perfect for plants. *Benjarong* (five colour) is a 16th-century Chinese treatment used on porcelain bowls, containers and fine china.

Lacquerware: It comes in two varieties: gleaming gold and black, and matte red with black and/or green details. Items include ornate containers and trays, wooden figurines, woven bamboo baskets and Burmese-style Buddhist manuscripts.

Fabrics: Shimmering Thai silk is made into a range of clothes and scarves as well as a wonderful range of contemporary furnishings, cushions and slippers. Thin *mud-mee* silk is from the Northeast, while the south is famous for its batik products; heavier cotton and linen is produced in Chiang Mai.

Gems and Jewellery: An important source of rubies and sapphires, Thailand is a world leader in cutting gems, and setting the stones in gold and silver in Thai and international designs. Burmese jade is carved into jewellery and *objets d'art*. Pearl farms in Phuket and Ko Samui create quality cultured pearls and pearl jewellery. A caveat: shop only at reputable stores.

Hill Tribe Crafts: The tribes of the northern hills produce brightly-coloured needlepoint work in geometric and floral patterns, used to decorate shirts, coats, bags and other items.

Although low in silver content, hill tribe silver is valued for its intricate craftsmanship and imaginative designs. There are ceremonial necklaces, headdresses, bracelets and rings, and knives, baskets, pipes and a gourd flute that sounds like a Scottish bagpipe.

Home Decorations: Thailand's artificial flowers and fruits made of fabric and paper

Left: colourful silk fabric
Right: wooden bookends

are virtually indistinguishable from fresh varieties. Street markets sell a huge variety of *sah* paper lanterns, linen bedspreads, mango and coconut wood kitchen utensils, and tiny papier mâché animals and boxes which are light and make great gifts.

Metal Art: Bronze deities, characters from the *Ramakien*, deer and abstract figures are cast up to 2m (6½ft) tall and clad in gleaming brass. Bronze is also crafted into cutlery. Silver and gold are pounded into jewellery and other decorative pieces, set with gems. Neillo ware receptacles are incised in silver or gold, the background cut away and an amalgam of dark metals used as filling, leaving the figures in high relief. Phuket tin is the prime ingredient in pewterware.

Cutting-edge Thai: Thai craftsmanship and creativity extend far beyond the realm of the traditional, and Bangkok is fast becoming a hub for cutting-edge design. Keep an eye out for Thailand's up-and-coming homegrown fashion labels, such as Fly Now and Jaspal, which have more flamboyant offerings, and Greyhound, with understated designs.

Thai designers are also making waves in the area of home decor. Propaganda (at Siam Discovery Centre and Emporium) stocks innovative accessories, while Ayodhya (at Gaysorn mall) offers unique furnishings made from water hyacinth. Thai cosmetics brands such as Harnn are also reinventing natural Thai beauty products like jasmine rice soap and tamarind facial scrubs, and packaging them in elegant rattan baskets.

WHERE TO BUY

Bangkok

Although Bangkok produces only a fraction of Thailand's arts and crafts, it is the country's main marketplace. There are huge air-conditioned malls filled with shops selling a wide variety of handicraft items. Some shopping centres are devoted to a single category of art products, like the **River City Shopping Complex**, which houses dozens of antiques shops, many with excellent replicas and real antiques. Queen Sirikit's **Chitralada** stores sell the rare crafts her organisation has worked so diligently to preserve. There are branches in the airport, Grand Palace, Oriental Plaza and

Pattaya. The Thai government's handicraft centre, **Narayana Phand**, at 127 Ratchadamri Road, displays the full selection. Silom, Surawong and Sukhumvit roads are lined with craft shops. Also worth a browse is **Sampeng Lane**, the **Thieves Market** and the **amulet markets** near Wat Mahathat and Wat Ratchanatda.

Suan Lum Night Bazaar and the huge weekend market at **Chatuchak** are also magnets for shoppers looking for arts and crafts and home accessories and clothing.

For luxury goods and designer labels, head for Bangkok's upmarket shopping centres, including **Siam Discovery Centre**, **Gaysorn**, **Emporium**, **Erawan Bangkok**, **Siam Paragon** and **Central World**, the largest shopping mall in Thailand. Edgier shopping enclaves like **Siam Square** and malls like **Mahboonkrong**, **Siam Centre** and **Playground** (in Soi Thonglor) cater for a younger and more funky crowd.

Chiang Mai

Shops along Borsang Road specialise in crafts; for quality silk furnishings, antiques and silk accessories, **Vila Cini** and **Oriental Collection** at 30 and 34 Charoenrat Road, have the widest range of quality goods. For cheap trinkets, the **night market** along Chang Khlan Road has hundreds of stalls.

Phuket and Ko Samui

At night, along the main beaches of Patong and Chaweng the souvenir stalls are endless. Prices are higher than Bangkok so try beating them down at least 20–50 percent.

Handicrafts sold here are usually of inferior quality, however local batik and printed sarongs from the south are popular. Beach pedlars sell hats, beads, T-shirts, wooden handicrafts and heavy silk counterpanes.

Above: bustling shoppers at the Mahboonkrong shopping centre

EATING OUT

Anyone who has tried Thai cuisine knows that it is among the best in the world, so make sure you sample it at its source. The country's Western restaurants are also among the finest and least expensive in Asia.

It is a fallacy that all Thai cuisine is extremely spicy. In truth, many Thais cannot stand very hot food and chefs will make any dish bland on request. Among the non-spicy dishes are: *thom kha gai* (coconut milk curry with chicken), *plaamuk thawd krathiem prik thai* (squid or fish fried with garlic and black pepper); *nua phat namman hoi* (beef in oyster sauce) and *hormok talay* (fish or seafood mousse).

Among the fiery favourites are *thom yam gung* (piquant soup with shrimp), *gaeng khiew wan gai* (a hot green curry with chicken or beef) and *gaeng phet* (a red curry with beef). Thais also make luscious sweets from coconut milk, tapioca and fruits. Some of the best are sold by street vendors. A plate of fresh Thai fruit is a delicious dessert.

Thai dishes are eaten with steamed white rice. Ladle some curry onto the rice and eat it before sampling the next curry so you do not obscure the unique flavour of each. The Thais eat with a fork in the left hand and a spoon in the right, using the fork to push the food onto the spoon.

The restaurants on the following pages are recommended as much for their atmosphere as for their superb food. Most restaurants close at 10pm; most hotel coffee shops at midnight. You can probably be seated without a reservation but call ahead to be sure.

Smoking is prohibited in public areas and air-conditioned public buildings, including restaurants and bars. Heavy penalties apply.

A general guide to prices for a dinner for one excluding beverage, tax and tips are:

$ = under 250 baht;
$$ = 250–750 baht;
$$$ = over 750 baht.

Bangkok

Baan Khanitha
36/1 Sukhumvit 23
Tel: 0-2258 4181
Always excellent Thai food served in a renovated Thai house decorated with antiques.

Right: Thai dishes at Sala Rim Naam

The menu includes a selection of *nam prik* or chili dips. Also has a second restaurant at 69 South Sathorn Road (tel: 0-2675 4200). *$$*

Basil
Sheraton Grande Sukhumvit
250 Sukhumvit Road
Tel: 0-2649 8888
Award-winning modern Thai restaurant serving home-style dishes located within this luxurious five-star hotel. Enjoy a lavish buffet lunch on Sunday. *$$$*

Biscotti
Four Seasons Hotel, 155 Ratchadamri Road
Tel: 0-2250 1000
This contemporary Italian restaurant wins accolades every year for its stylish ambience, great Italian food and fine wines. *$$$*

Blue Elephant
233 South Sathorn Road
Tel: 0-2673 9353/6
Internationally famous for its Royal Thai cuisine, this classic restaurant and cookery school is located in a beautiful colonial mansion. *$$–$$$*

Eat Me!
1/6 Soi Piphat 2, off Convent Road, Silom
Tel: 0-2238 0931
Trendy crowds fill this laid-back Australian-Thai restaurant every night, tucked away from the busy Soi Convent. Serves clever and innovative fusion cuisine. The restaurant also hosts occasional art exhibitions. *$$–$$$*

Hazara
29 Sukhumvit Soi 38
Tel: 0-2713 6048/9
Find excellent Indian food at this most popular section of The Face's compound, which

also houses the Lan Na Thai restaurant and the popular Face Bar.

Manohra Song Sunset Dinner Cruise
Departures daily from Bangkok Marriott Resort & Spa
Tel: 0-2477 0770
www.manohracruises.com
A former rice barge takes guests on an evening cruise along the river with a Thai dinner served on board; the boat leaves every evening at 7.30pm, returning at 10pm. *$$$*

Mezzaluna
65th Floor, State Tower Bangkok
1055 Silom Road
Tel: 0-2624 9555
Enjoy high-end Italian cuisine high up in the sky, with the view of the Chao Phraya River. Also try the 63rd-floor Sirocco restaurant (outdoor; international) and Sky Bar (outdoor; cocktails) and 64th-floor Distil (indoor, outdoor – wine and cigar bar). *$$$*

Sala Rim Naam
Oriental Hotel, 48 Oriental Avenue
Tel: 0-2437 6211
Located in a beautiful, temple-like building across the river from the Oriental Hotel. Particularly good classical Thai dancing, performed before your table every night. Free boat service is provided from the Oriental's boat landing. *$$$*

Supatra River House
226 Soi Wat Rakhang, Arunamarin Road
Tel: 0-2411 0305
This old riverside house offers excellent Thai food in a stylish and elegant setting; Friday and Saturday evening dinner shows with Thai dancing. *$$*

To Die For
998 Soi Thonglor, Sukhumvit Soi 55
Tel: 0-2381 4714
Trendy New York-style restaurant and bar in the hip H1 shopping mall. Tasty international cuisine amid background house music. *$$$*

Whole Earth
71 Sukhumvit Soi 26
Tel: 0-2258 4900
Dine Thai-style (ie, on the floor) at this popular restaurant serving delicious Thai vegetarian dishes at very reasonable prices. It has a branch in Soi Lang Suan (tel: 0-2252 5574), close to Lumphini Park. *$–$$*

Ayutthaya
Baan Watcharachai
9 Moo 7, Tambon Ban Pom
near Wat Kasatrathirat
Tel: 0-3532 1333
A floating riverside restaurant with a river terrace and a quiet garden with Thai pavilions. Limited English spoken. *$*

Hua Hin
Chao Ley
15 Naresdamri Road
Tel: 0-3251 3436
This old-timer is one of several seafood restaurants on the pier, and serves some of the freshest fish in town. *$–$$*

Mamma Mia
19 Damneon Kasem Road
Tel: 0-3253 3636
Run by Milan native Claudio, this authentic Italian eatery has a pizzeria upstairs while authentic Italian dishes are served downstairs. *$$–$$$*

Supatra-by-the-sea
122/63 Takiab Road
Tel: 0-3253 6561
Right at the end of Hua Hin beach, this lovely restaurant is a sister establishment of the hugely popular Supatra River House in Bangkok. Expect well-executed Thai dishes served on the torch-lit garden terrace or up in the main pavilion. *$$*

Pattaya
Lobster Pot
288 Walking Street
Tel: 0-3842 6083
Pattaya's finest seafood restaurant has an extensive menu with an equally good wine list. *$$$*

Mantra Restaurant & Bar
240 Moo 5, Pattaya Beach Road
Tel: 0-3842 9591
Serves an interesting mix of Asian (Thai, Japanese, Chinese, Indian) and Mediter-

- thanks to its delicious international fare and wide drinks list. $$

Le Grand Lanna
51/4 Moo 1, San Kampaeng Road
Tel: 0-5326 2569
Excellent Lanna restaurant and cooking school set in delightful grounds, among lily ponds and pavilions. $$

Old Chiang Mai Cultural Center
185/3 Wualai Road
Tel: 0-5320 2993/5
Known for its traditional Northern style *khantoke* dinner accompanied by classic Thai and hill tribe dance shows. $$

Phuket Laikhram
1/10 Suthep Road
Tel: 0-5327 8909
An excellent restaurant serving Southern Thai dishes, from various curries to *thom yam*-style noodles. $

ranean dishes. Later in the evening, it turns into a nightspot that plays chill-out music. $$–$$$

PIC Kitchen
Pattaya 2 Road, Soi 5
Tel: 0-3842 8387
Thai food served at low tables in traditional style, with vening classical Thai dancing. $$

Chiang Mai
Gallery Bar & Restaurant
25–9 Charoenrat Road
Tel: 0-5324 8601/2
Exquisite Lanna decor and great art exhibitions from local craftspeople are complemented by Central and Northern style cooking on the river at local prices. $

Good View Pub & Restaurant
13 Charoenrat Road (opposite petrol station)
Tel: 0-5324 1866
Hopping live music venue right by the river. Menu includes Japanese, Thai and Western food; very lively at night. $$

Huen Penn
112 Ratchamankha Road
Tel: 0-5327 7103
Delicious Northern Thai specialities have given this small restaurant a big name so come early, especially at lunchtime when locals fill the tables. No credit cards. $

Le Coq D'Or
68/1 Ko Klang Road, Nong Hoi
Tel: 0-5328 2024 or 0-5380 1501
This former British Consular residence has been pulling in the crowds for over 30 years

Chiang Rai
Mae Ui Khiaw
1064/1 Sanam Bin Road
Tel: 0-5375 3173
One of the best places to sample simple Northern-style cooking in quiet, unassuming surrounds. $

Muang Thong Phattakan
Phahonyothin Road
Tel: 0-5371 162
Simple but excellent authentic Chinese-Thai dishes including the wholesome rice soup known as *khao tom* with either pork, fish or chicken. $

Mae Hong Son
Fern Restaurant
87 Khunlumpraphat Road
Tel: 0-5361 1374
This rustic restaurant near Jong Kum Lake is one of the town's best. The typically spicy dishes are cooked with a deft touch and are not too overpowering. $

Thip Restaurant
23/1 Praditjongkham Road
Tel: 0-5362 0553
One of the few good lakeside venues that

Above: open-air terrace dining in Chiang Mai

are actually on the water, serving simple Northern-style food. Very popular with locals and tourists. $

Phuket

Al Dente
Patak Road, Karon Beach
Tel: 0-7639 6596
One of the best places for homemade Italian pizza and pasta served in a buzzing atmosphere with plenty of charm. $$

Baan Rim Pa
100/7 Kalim Beach Road, Patong
Tel: 0-7634 0789
Probably Phuket's best Thai restaurant, located on a cliff-top at Patong beach's northern end. In addition to excellent cuisine, it offers elegant decor and magnificent views. Reservations essential. $$$

Chez Serge
Burasari Resort
32/1 Soi Ruam Jai, Patong Beach
Tel: 0-7629 2929
Famous for once catering to Bangkok starlets and royalty, this popular French–Thai-run restaurant has moved from Phuket Town to its new location near the beach. $$

Kan Eang I
44/1 Viset Road, Chalong Bay
Tel: 0-7638 1212
Popular alfresco seafood restaurant with two branches (I and II) specialising in delicious lobster, crab and giant prawns. $$

Kata Mama
South end of Kata Yai Beach
Tel: 0-7628 4301
This family-run operation serving home-style Thai dishes is a huge favourite. Try the fried fish with garlic and pepper, and barbecued prawns with chilli sauce. $–$$

On the Rock
Marina Phuket Resort
47 Karon Road, Karon Beach
Tel: 0-7633 0625
Great setting on the rocky promontory overlooking Karon Beach with a wide choice of fresh seafood as well as superb views. $$

Salvatores
15–17 Rasada Road, Phuket Town
Tel: 0-7622 5958
Tatler Thailand voted this the country's best Italian restaurant. Try the gnocchi with lamb sauce and homemade ice-cream. Reservations recommended. $$–$$$

Krabi

Azura Nova
142 Ao Nang Beach
Tel: 0-7563 7848
Lovely Mediterranean ambience with tiled floors, marble tables and vines creeping up the walls. Owned by Italians; the food is as authentic as it can get. $$–$$$

Ruen Mai
Maharat Road
Tel: 0-7563 1797
Staff can prepare, on request, meat-free versions of any dish on the menu. Try the stir-fried *sataw* ('stinky beans') in red curry paste, and wing bean spicy salad. $–$$

Ko Samui

Betelnut
43/04 Moo 3, Soi Colibri, Chaweng Beach
Tel: 0-7741 3370
Owned by American Jeffrey Lord, the restaurant's design is simple but tasteful, leaving the focus on the small but innovative selection of Californian-meets-Thai fusion fare. $$$

The Islander
Central Chaweng Beach
Tel: 0-7723 0836
The menu has an extensive range of international favourites. Look out for the daily specials. Several TVs screen sports. $$

Rice
91/1 Moo 2, Chaweng Beach
Tel: 0-7723 1934
This split-level international and Thai restaurant has a large lily pond in front and a glass elevator to carry diners up to the third level where a more exclusive gourmet experience awaits at the rooftop Rice & Stars. $$$

Above: pineapple rice

NIGHTLIFE
Bangkok

Bangkok by night glitters with upscale restaurants, clubs, open-air beer gardens with live bands, pubs and cabaret shows, offering hundreds of options for all ages and tastes. Many of the nightspots change regularly as trends come and go, but there are some old favourites that keep on going, thanks to their consistently good music and great entertainment.

The bad news is that, in 2001, the government introduced a New Social Order Campaign with draconian policing of entertainment venues and confusing Nightlife Zoning laws to clamp down on rampant drug abuse and under-age drinking. Three nightlife zones were designated – Silom Road, Ratchada-phisek Road and Royal City Avenue (RCA) – in which venues with valid dance licences can stay open until 2am. The rest must close at 1am. In addition, during occasional police raids, when revellers are urine-tested for drugs, the police may ask foreigners to show their passports – or face a fine. Many clubs won't let visitors in without one. To get around the miserably early closing time, do as what most Thais are forced to do: start your evening early, say by 10.30pm, so there is ample time to wind down by the time the clubs close.

Bars, Pubs and Live Music
Diplomat Bar
Conrad Hotel, 87 Witthayu (Wireless) Road
Tel: 0-2690 9999
This elegant bar is most popular with business executives for after-hour cocktails. Jazz nightly and great ambience.

Distil
State Tower, Silom Road
Tel: 0-2624 9555
Part of the Dome complex on the 64th floor of State Tower building, this chic bar allows you a choice of some 2,000 wines. Lie back on the outdoor balcony sofa cushions and enjoy.

Met Bar
Metropolitan Hotel, Sathorn Road
Tel: 0-2625 3399
Equalling the panache of London's trendy Met Bar, Bangkok's younger sister at the Metropolitan is one of the capital's most exclusive yet friendly nightspots. The dark, intimate members-only bar has resident and visiting international DJs.

Syn Bar
Swissôtel Nai Lert Park Hotel
2 Witthayu (Wireless) Road
Tel: 0-2253 0123
This former hotel lobby bar has been dramatically transformed into a retro-chic cocktail lounge by a New York designer. The all-female bartenders mix up some devilishly tasty cocktails and flavoured martinis.

V9
Sofitel Silom, 188 Silom Road
Tel: 0-2238 1991
Chic wine bar and restaurant on the 37th floor with some of the best views of the city. Buy wine for immediate consumption from its cellar (no charge for corkage). Live music alternates with DJ-spun tunes.

Dance Clubs
Bed Supperclub
26 Sukhumvit Soi 11
Tel: 0-2651 3537
www.bedsupperclub.com
Located next door to the hip restaurant of the same name. Dance the night away or lounge on huge beds scattered around the ground and mezzanine levels. Jazz, funk and techno.

Narcissus
112 Sukhumvit Soi 23
Tel: 0-2241 3991

Right: trendy Bed Supperclub

One of the city's biggest and best clubs with fancy lights, decor and sound system, topped by a glitter globe hanging over the dance floor.

Q Bar
34 Sukhumvit Soi 11
Tel: 0-2252 3274
www.qbarbangkok.com
Groovy multi-level bar with upstairs balcony; its dance floor is packed at weekends with out-of-towners and Thai regulars.

Tapas
114/17 Silom Road, Soi 4
Tel: 0-2632 0920
Arguably the hottest dance floor downtown, this award-winning club still keeps pumping out the good tunes. Packed with expats and twenty-something locals.

Gay and Lesbian Venues
DJ Station
8/6–8 Silom Soi 2
Tel: 0-2266 4029
Bangkok's most popular gay club is packed throughout the night. The atmosphere is electric and patrons often dress outrageously.

Hua Hin
Hua Hin's nightlife is subdued compared to Bangkok, but there are a few local bars outside of hotels. Most visitors enjoy the beachside restaurants.

Bars, Pubs and Live Music
Hua Hin Brewing Company
Hilton Hua Hin Resort & Spa
33 Naresdamri Road
Tel: 0-3253 8999
Enormous bar, restaurant and disco run by the Hilton with DJs nightly until late. Brews its own beer on the premises.

Jungle Juice Bar & Restaurant
19/1 Selakam Road
Tel: 0-6167 7120
This friendly, low-key place is a favourite with expats. Serves Brit-style pub grub.

Pattaya
Pattaya's nightlife scene is legendary. Unfortunately, most of it, centring around girlie bars and commercial sex, is rather sleazy.

Hotels have lobby bands and bars with lounge singers. Beach Road and Pattaya 2 Road are lined with beer bars, which differ little from their cousins in South Pattaya.

Chiang Mai
Chiang Mai's nightlife is centred around the Night Bazaar and near Tape Gate.

Bars, Pubs and Live Music
Good View Pub & Restaurant
13 Charoenrat Road
Tel: 0-5324 1866
Solo artistes and rock 'n roll bands play nightly in this riverside pub and restaurant.

Sax Bar
35/2 Moon Muang Road
Tel: 0-5321 9432
A predominantly bohemian hangout for those who prefer eclectic mood music from a DJ and a very arty atmosphere.

Dance Clubs
Space Bubble Discotheque
Pornping Tower Hotel
Tel: 0-5327 0099
One of the oldest nightclubs in town giving young locals and travellers a chance to groove to mainly techno sounds.

Phuket
In high season, Phuket's few clubs centred around Patong Beach are packed to the rafters. Kata and Karon have fewer options.

Bars, Pubs and Live Music
Molly Malone's
91/1 Thaweewong Road, Patong
Tel: 0-7629 2771/2
Popular Irish pub with live bands nightly and good food catering to expats and tourists.

The Green Man
82/15 Pratak Road, Rawai
Tel: 0-7628 0757
This English country-style pub is much sought after by those not based in Patong.

Dance Clubs
Banana Disco
Thaweewong Road, Patong
Tel: 0-7634 0301

Patong's longest established disco also has an open-air pub to relax in.

Safari Pub and Disco
28 Siriat Road, Patong Hill
Tel: 0-7634 1079
Outdoor safari-themed disco with waterfalls, jungle vines and loud, intense music.

Cabaret
Simon Cabaret
8 Sirirach Road, Patong
Tel: 0-7634 2011
www.phuket-simoncabaret.com
This has evolved into a professional show-piece, with elaborate stage sets and a few comic laughs. Shows are performed every evening at 7.30pm and 9.30pm.

Phuket Fantasea
99 Moo 3 Kamala Beach
Tel: 0-7638 5000
www.phuket-fantasea.com
A huge cultural theme park that explores Thailand's 'Myths, Mysteries and Magic'. Offers a dinner buffet with the show. Open Friday to Wednesday 5.30pm–11.30pm.

Krabi
The nightlife is quiet but Ao Nang has a few bars catering for budget travellers.

Irish Rover Bar and Grill
247/8 Moo 2, Ao Nang Beach
Tel: 0-7563 7607
Convivial Irish-style pub with Guinness flowing all evening and sports on overhead TVs.

Luna Beach Bar
Ao Nang Beach
Hip dance bar with pool tables, DJs and a lively atmosphere. Puts on regular all-night raves for the 'full moon' dance fanatics.

Ko Samui
Most entertainment outlets are centred around the Lamai and Chaweng areas.

Bars, Pubs and Live Music
Ark Bar
Chaweng Beach
Tel: 0-7742 2047
www.ark-bar.com
A bar and restaurant with a mainly Brit clientele. The dance music picks up from early evening onwards.

Gecko Village
Bo Phut Beach
Tel: 0-7724 5554
www.geckosamui.com
Features some of Ko Samui's best DJ-spun dance beats, with big international names making guest appearances.

Green Mango
Soi Green Mango, Chaweng Beach
Tel: 0-7742 2148
Huge venue that is crammed on most nights. The music is mainstream Euro-dance.

Tropical Murphy's
14/40 Chaweng Beach Road
Tel: 0-7741 3614
www.tropicalmurphys.com
This traditional Irish pub is the only one of its kind on the island. The music ranges from dance, blues, disco, jazz to Irish.

Zico's
38/2 Moo 3, Chaweng Beach Road
Tel: 0-7723 1560/3
It's no Rio, but here you can find Brazilian churrascaria barbecue, samba music and a carnival atmosphere.

Above: Phuket nightlights

CALENDAR OF EVENTS

Plan your visit to coincide with a Thai festival. Thais celebrate even their religious holidays with gusto and encourage visitors to join in. Check with the Tourism Authority of Thailand (TAT) for exact dates as these may vary from year to year.

January
Borsang Umbrella Fair (Chiang Mai): Mid-month. This colourful festival honours the craftsmen who make Chiang Mai's beautiful umbrellas. Parades, cultural presentations and craft demonstrations are held.

February
Flower Festival (Chiang Mai): Flowers are abloom at this time of the year in the cool air and flower exhibitions are staged. The key event is a grand floral procession through the streets of the city, with floats, marching bands and the beautiful people of Chiang Mai. Early February.
Makha Puja (nationwide): Celebrates the gathering of 1,200 disciples to hear Buddha

preach. As the full moon rises, buy incense sticks, a candle and flowers, and join a candlelight procession around a Buddhist temple. After completing three circuits, place your candle, incense sticks and flowers in the sand-filled trays, make a *wai* (hands clasped in prayer before the face) and depart. Full moon night.
Kite-flying season (Bangkok): At Sanam Luang, next to Wat Phra Kaew, kids fly kites of every shape and colour while older Thais compete in ancient kite battles. The season runs through April.

April
Poy Sang Long (Mae Hong Son and Chiang Mai): Young Shan boys are ordained into the Buddhist monkhood. Unlike in other parts of Thailand, here they are dressed in the most elaborate costumes. Early April.
Songkran (nationwide): The traditional Thai New Year when one blesses friends by sprinkling water on them. It quickly develops into a fun, full-scale war with ample dousings. Expect to get drenched and dress appropriately. Chiang Mai (along the banks of the Ping River) and the small towns have the rowdiest action. 13–15 April.

May
Loy Rua (Phuket): A sea gypsy festival where fishermen build 2½-m (8-ft) long model boats of bamboo and fill them with models of weapons as well as strands of hair, fingernail clippings and other items where bad luck is believed to reside. Full moon days.
Visakha Puja (nationwide): Commemorates Buddha's birth, enlightenment and death, which all occurred on the same day. It is celebrated in the same manner as Magha Puja. Full moon night.
The Royal Ploughing Ceremony (Sanam Luang, Bangkok): An ancient, brilliantly colourful ceremony presided over by the Crown Prince to mark the beginning of the rice-planting season. Buy tickets at the TAT office. Mid-month.

July
Asarnha Puja (nationwide): Commemorates Buddha's first sermon to his first five disciples. It is celebrated in the same manner as Makha Puja. Full moon night.

Above: Makha Puja festival at Bangkok's Wat Benjamabophit
Right: casting away bad luck, Loy Krathong festival

September

Chinese Moon Festival (nationwide): The Chinese celebrate the Moon Festival by placing small shrines laden with fruit, incense and candles in front of their homes to honour the moon goddess. A lovely festival, highlighted by the eating of scrumptious cakes shaped like full moons. Found at no other time of the year, these mooncakes are filled with a paste made of either red bean or lotus seed. Full moon night of the eighth lunar month.

International Swan Boat Races (Bangkok): Held under Bangkok's Rama IX Bridge. Draws participants from all around the world. Mid-month.

Vegetarian Festival (Phuket): This is the most unusual of Phuket's festivals. There are daily street processions but its most salient features are tests of devotion that are definitely not for the squeamish. Devotees put themselves into a trance before performing feats of daring including climbing ladders with rungs made of knives, running skewers, hoses, spears and even Chiang Mai umbrellas through cheeks and tongues, and, the most daring of all, walking barefoot across fiery coals. Chinese opera and vegetarian food are offered at temples. To enter the temples, dress entirely in white. Mid-month, but sometimes in October.

October

Chonburi Buffalo Races (Chonburi province): Water buffaloes and their farm boy jockeys race for prizes. Late October.

November

Loy Krathong (nationwide): The most beautiful of Thai celebrations. Thais (and foreigners) launch tiny candle-bearing boats in streams and ponds to wash away sins and bless love affairs. It is a romantic night for lovers of all ages. Sukhothai, where the festival reputedly started in the 13th century, is the most beautiful place to witness proceedings. Full moon night.

December

Trooping of the Colours (Bangkok): Two days before his birthday, the king reviews his colourful regiments at the Rama V Plaza. Get tickets at TAT offices. 3 December.

Phuket King's Cup Regatta (Phuket): A long-distance yacht race which has become a fixture on international yachting calendars. Centred at Nai Harn beach. Early December.

Chiang Mai Winter Fair (Chiang Mai): The annual winter fair offers cultural and handicraft shows, the 'Miss Chiang Mai' contest and a product fair at the Municipal Stadium. Late December.

Practical
Information

GETTING THERE

By Air
Suvarnabhumi (pronounced 'su-wan-na-poom') **Airport**, also known as the **New Bangkok International Airport** (NBIA), replaced Don Muang airport in September 2006. Approximately 30km (19 miles) east of the city, the new airport boasts the largest terminal and tallest control tower in the world. (For information, see www.bangkokairportonline.com.) Several airlines fly direct from Australasia, Europe and the US. Thailand has five other international airports: Chiang Mai, Hat Yai, Phuket, Samui and Sukhothai.

The national airline Thai Airways International (www.thaiairways.com) flies to over 50 cities all over the world. **Bangkok Airways** (www.bangkokair.com) is an excellent regional airline with exclusive routes within Asia.

By Rail
An overnight train to Laos stops on the Thai border at Nong Khai, while another rail link connects Thailand with Singapore, via Butterworth in Malaysia.

By Road
From Malaysia, travel either by taxi or by tour buses. These connect Singapore and Malaysia with Hat Yai in southern Thailand.

TRAVEL ESSENTIALS

When to Visit
The cool season, from mid-November to mid-February, is the best time to visit. However, bear in mind that during Christmas, New Year and Chinese New Year (January/February), hotels tend to be full and room rates go up.

Visas & Passports
Visitors from many countries, including the UK and US, are issued 30-day free entry permits on arrival. Tourist visas for 60- and 90-day stays are available outside the country, depending on one's nationality. It is advisable to check with a Thai embassy or consulate before your departure. See www.mfa.go.th/web/12.php for information.

The 30-day entry permits can be extended for up to 10 days for a fee. All visas can be extended for a fee at immigration offices (tel: 0-2287 3101; www.immigration.go.th).

Customs
Thailand bans firearms, pornographic materials and drugs. Cash imports of over US$10,000 must be declared. The Bangkok Airport has a green and red customs channel and any searches are brief and polite. For more information, see www.customs.go.th.

Vaccinations
Although the chance of contracting them is very slim, polio, rabies, Japanese encephalitis and typhoid fever vaccinations are recommended. Anyone arriving from a yellow fever area must carry a certificate attesting to recent inoculation.

Weather
Bangkok's weather is slightly different from the rest of the country; seasons are as follows: **Hot**: March–mid-June, 27–35°C (80–95°F); **Rainy**: June –October, 24–32°C (75–90°F); **Cool**: November–February, 18–32°C (65–90°F) with lower humidity.

Chiang Mai enjoys a cooler climate. In the cool season, temperatures range 13–28°C (55–82°F) and are lower in the hills.

Left: river transport between Laos and Thailand. **Right:** immigration check

In **Phuket** and places along the **Andaman Coast**, the monsoon season is from early May to late October. Temperatures range from 34°C (93°F) in the hot season to night-time temperatures of 21°C (70°F) in the cool season.

The **southern Gulf of Thailand** around Ko Samui has intermittent rain from May to October, but the wettest season is from November to January.

What to Wear

Clothes should be light and loose; natural fibres or blends are recommended. Sunglasses are essential; hats protect heads on sunny days. Shorts are taboo at temples and mosques. Shoes must be removed upon entering temple buildings. Winter nights in north Thailand can be chilly so pack warm clothing.

Electricity

Electricity is rated at 220 volts, 50 cycles. Generally, dual flat-pronged plugs are used.

Time Zone

Thailand is seven hours ahead of GMT.

GETTING ACQUAINTED

Geography

At 514,000sq km (198,455sq miles), Thailand is approximately the size of France. Bangkok, the nation's capital, is divided by the Chao Phraya River into twin cities – Bangkok and Thonburi. It covers an area of 1,565sq km (604sq miles).

Thailand's second largest city, Chiang Mai, lies 696km (432 miles) north of Bangkok and sits 313m (1,027ft) above sea level, crowned by the 1,073-m (3,520-ft)-high Doi Suthep.

Phuket, an island in the Andaman Sea, lies 890km (553 miles) from Bangkok. Measuring 48.7km (30 miles) long by 21.3km (13 miles) wide, it is roughly the size of Singapore.

Government and Economy

Thailand is a constitutional monarchy with power vested in a House of Representatives and a Senate, both elected by popular vote. The executive branch comprises a coalition of political parties which select a prime minister who rules through a Cabinet. Thailand has an independent judiciary.

Thailand enjoys a free-enterprise economy. Tourism is a top foreign exchange earner, followed by agricultural produce and commodities. In the late 1980s, the country embarked on an industrialisation programme which transformed the countryside and helped record annual double digit GNP growth. It has a well-developed telecommunications, road and power infrastructure. Thailand's economy took a sharp downturn in mid-1997, but the former prime minister, Thaksin Shinawatra – voted into power in 2001 and in 2005 – pursued populist policies that helped get the economy back on track.

Religion

About 92 percent of the population are Buddhists. Five percent are Muslims, most of whom inhabit the south. The rest of the population are Christian, Hindu or Sikh. Hill tribes practise animism, but the Karens and Lahu have converted to Christianity.

How Not To Offend

The royal family is regarded with genuine reverence. Insults to the royal family is one area where Thais show little tolerance, so avoid making any disrespectful remarks and always stand when the Royal Anthem is played, including at cinemas.

Disrespect towards Buddha images, temples or monks is not taken lightly either. Monks observe strict vows of chastity that prohibit their being touched by women, even their mothers.

Thais believe that the head is a sacred fount of wisdom, so it is insulting to touch another person on the head. Using foot gestures is considered rude; never point your feet at or step over a person.

Left: Krabi countryside

Population

Thailand has a population of over 65 million people, about 75 percent of whom are ethnic Thai. The Chinese, who comprise 12 to 15 percent of the population, represent the largest ethnic minority in the country. Thai Malays of the south make up about 2 percent of the population, and the tribal groups of the northern hills another 1 percent.

Bangkok holds some 10 million people, almost a third of whom are migrants.

MONEY MATTERS

Currency

The Thai baht, is divided into 100 satangs. Banknote denominations include 1,000B, 500B, 100B, 50B and 20B. There are 10B, 5B, 1B, 50-satang and 25-satang coins. At the time of writing, the baht was trading at 37 to the US dollar. For daily rates, check the *Bangkok Post* or *The Nation* newspapers. Government rates are also posted at banks and exchange kiosks.

Credit Cards

Amex, Diners Club, MasterCard and Visa are widely accepted throughout Bangkok, Chiang Mai, Phuket and major up-country towns. Expect a surcharge of between 3 and 5 percent on their use at some outlets, especially travel agents.
Amex, tel: 0-2273 5222
Diners, tel: 0-2238 3660
MasterCard, tel: 001-800-11-887 0663
Visa, tel: 001-800-441 3485

Tipping

Most good restaurants, especially those that cater for foreigners, add a service charge to the bill. In ordinary restaurants outside of tourist zones, a tip of 10 to 15 percent would be appreciated. There is no tipping for taxis or *tuk tuk*, although rounding up the fare to the next even number will be appreciated.

GETTING AROUND

From the Airport

Bangkok: Bangkok's new Suvarnabhumi Airport is linked to the city by a convenient system of elevated highways. Road travel from the airport to most parts of Bangkok averages 45 minutes.

Air-conditioned, metered public taxis are found on Level 1 of the Arrival Hall. Arrange for a taxi at one of the taxi desks. At the end of your trip, pay the amount on the meter plus a 50-baht airport surcharge. If the driver uses the expressway, the toll fees will add up to 60 baht.

Air-conditioned airport limousines (using Mercedes and Toyota cars) have desks at the airport but these cost considerably more.

Special airport buses – outside the Arrival Hall – go to many central destinations in the city. Departures are every 15 minutes and tickets cost 150 baht.

Chiang Mai: The airport is a 10-minute drive from the city centre. Major hotels have vans that ferry guests door to door. A THAI mini-van runs between the airport and its office at 240 Phra Pokklao Road.

Phuket: The airport is 30km (19 miles), or a 45-minute drive, from Phuket Town. If you haven't made arrangements with your hotel to pick you up, THAI Ground Services offer air-conditioned taxis to various beaches and there are many private minibus services to Phuket Town and Patong.

Taxis

Bangkok's taxis are mostly new and air-conditioned and metered. Make sure the driver switches the meter on at the start of the ride. The flag fall is 35 baht. There is no extra charge for baggage handling, stowage or extra passengers. No tipping is required. There are no taxi stands; just wave down a passing taxi. Avoid parked taxis as they usually ask more than those you flag down. Taxi drivers' command of English is often limited.

Tuk-tuk

Tuk-tuk are the small, three-wheeled motorised taxis whose name derives from the rattling noise of their engines. In most tourist areas, drivers speak some English. Fares begin at 70 baht in Bangkok, but in Chiang Mai and Phuket, the starting price is 50 baht. *Samlor*, the pedal trishaws, charge 40 baht for short distances. Bargain before you board.

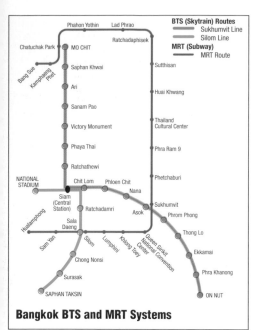

Bangkok BTS and MRT Systems

Motorcycle taxis

In **Bangkok**, you will see locals taking motorcycle taxis in heavy traffic. Though useful and cheap for short trips down narrow lanes, the high incidence of accidents is forcing a government crack-down. Helmets are mandatory.

In **Chiang Mai**, motorcycle taxis run up the Mae Sa Valley road, passing the elephant camp and orchid farms. In **Phuket**, motorcycle taxis leave from the market on Ranong Road. Drivers in maroon vests convey passengers anywhere in the town centre for 20–30 baht per ride.

Buses

Bangkok: Blue-and-white air-conditioned buses cover over a dozen routes in the city. Ordinary red-and-white and blue-and-white buses operate more than 120 routes. The route numbers of air-conditioned buses don't correspond with those of ordinary buses.

Green mini-buses are smaller but their route numbers correspond to those of ordinary buses since they ply the same routes.

Phuket: Wooden buses leave every 30 minutes between 8am and 6pm from Phuket Town market for all beaches. Buses to Rawai

and Nai Harn, however, leave from the roundabout on Bangkok Road. Flag one down. Tuk-tuks run between Patong and Karon/Kata beaches; negotiate a fare before you set off.

Chiang Mai: There is no proper bus service in the city; the best way to get around is by flagging down a taxi, or one of the many red *songthaew* (pick-up trucks) that ply the streets. They are usually willing to take you anywhere and can be hired for half-day or whole-day trips into the countryside.

Skytrain

The **Bangkok Transit System**'s elevated train service, better known as the Skytrain, covers an inner city area of 24-km (15-miles). It comprises two main lines, the Sukhumvit Line and the Silom Line, which intersect at Siam Station.

The skytrain runs from 6am to midnight every day, with rides costing between 10 and 40 baht. Tourists may find it more useful to buy the unlimited ride 1-day Pass (100 baht) or the 30-day Adult Pass, which comes in three types: 250 baht, 10 rides; 300 baht, 15 rides, and 540 baht, 30 rides.

BTS Tourist Information Centres are at Nana, Siam and Saphan Taksin stations (daily 8am–8pm). Further information is available on the BTS hotline, tel: 0-2617 6000 or www.bts.co.th.

MRT (Subway)

Bangkok's 20-km (12-mile) subway line has 18 stations and links major areas not covered by the BTS, such as Hualamphong, Asok, Lat Phrao, Ratchadaphisek, Chatuchak Park and Phahon Yothin. Travellers can connect between the BTS and MRTA at Sukhumvit, Silom and Chatuchak Park stations. Fares range from 14 to 36 baht. Further information is available at tel: 0-2624 5744 or www.bangkokmetro.co.th.

River Transport

In **Bangkok**, the **Chao Phraya River Express Boat** (tel: 0-2623 6143; www.chaophrayaboat.co.th) travels between Tha Nonthaburi pier in the north and Tha Wat Rachasingkhon near Krungthep Bridge in the south. Boats run every 15 minutes from 6am to 7.55pm, and stop at different piers according to the coloured flag on the top of the boat. Fares range from 9 baht to 15 baht and are paid on board or at some pier counters.

Yellow-flag boats are the fastest and do not stop at many piers, while the orange-flag and no-flag boats stop at most of the marked river piers. Express boats are packed during rush hours so make sure you keep a firm grip on your valuables.

The **Chao Phraya Tourist Boat** (www. chaophrayaboat.co.th) is a large cruiser that follows a fixed route to and from the Central (Tha Sathorn) Pier, along some of the river's major tourist sites. This user-friendly 'hop-on and hop-off' service costs 100 baht per ticket and allows unlimited rides from 9.30am until 3pm. After 3pm, the same ticket can be used on the regular express boats.

Car Hire

All big cities offer car hire from major international companies or local agents. Bring along some photo ID and a valid International Drivers' Licence. Islands and rural cities often have 4WD vehicles available. Always check the vehicle has proper insurance and Collision Damage Waiver (CDW). Expect to pay a deposit, as well as an extra fee of around 1,500 baht for drop-off in another city. Automatic cars are charged approximately 150 baht extra.
Avis, tel: 0-2251 1131; avisthailand.com
Budget, tel: 0-2203 9200; www.budget.co.th
Hertz, www.hertz.com

Motorcycle Hire

Motorcycle hire is not advisable in **Bangkok** due to erratic driving and poor safety standards. Resort towns offer models varying from small bikes to heavy roadsters. Few offer any insurance so careful driving and personal travel insurance is advisable.

Inter-City Rail

The State Railways of Thailand (tel: 0-2222 0175) operates five principal routes from Bangkok's **Hualamphong Station**. Trains are clean, cheap and reliable. View routes, timetables and fares on www.railway.co.th.

Another line leaves **Bangkok Noi** (tel: 0-2411 3100) station in Thonburi for Kanchanaburi and other destinations in the west.

Inter-City Bus

The inexpensive long-distance bus network and slightly pricier VIP and Super VIP coach service are used by locals, and provide a cheap and sometimes faster alternative to train travel. All buses are operated by the **Transport Company Ltd** (tel: 0-2576 5599; www.transport.co.th). The terminals are:
Eastern Bus Station (tel: 0-2391 2504) is at Sukhumvit, Soi Ekamai (Ekamai BTS).
North and Northeastern Bus Station (tel: 0-2936 2853) is at Kamphaeng Phet Road I (Mo Chit BTS). **Southern Bus Station** (tel: 0-2435 1199, 0-2434 7192) is at Boromrat Chaonanani Road, Thonburi (ask taxis for Sai Tai Mai).

Domestic Airlines

Thai Airways International (THAI; www. thaiairways.com) operates domestic flights to 11 major cities and towns in Thailand using a fleet of 737s and Airbuses. Other airlines serving domestic destinations are: **Bangkok Airways** (www.bangkokair.com), **Nok Air** (www.nokair.co.th), **Orient Thai** (www. orient-thai.com; www.fly12go.com) and **AirAsia** (www.airasia.com).

HOURS AND HOLIDAYS

Business Hours

Business hours are Monday to Friday 8.30am–5.30pm. Some businesses are open on Saturday from 8.30am to noon. Government offices are open from Monday to Friday 8.30am–4.30pm. Banks are open from Monday to Friday 8.30am–3.30pm. Many Thai banks operate street money-changing kiosks which are open daily 8.30am–8pm. Department stores are open daily from approximately 10am to 10pm.

Right: Bangkok's Skytrain

Public Holidays

New Year's Day	1 January
Makha Puja	February full moon
Chakri Day	6 April
Songkran	12–14 April
Labour Day	1 May
Coronation Day	5 May
Visakha Puja	May full moon
Asarnha Puja	July full moon
HM the Queen's Birthday	12 August
Democracy Day	14 October
Chulalongkorn Day	23 October
HM the King's Birthday	5 December
Constitution Day	10 December
New Year's Eve	31 December

Chinese New Year: January/February (date determined by lunar calendar); not officially recognised as a holiday, but many shops close for four days.

ACCOMMODATION

Thailand has a wide range of hotels (some of which are consistently ranked the world's best) to suit different budgets. Add 10 percent service charge and 7 percent value-added tax to the prices. It is acceptable to bargain, especially during the low season (May to October). Price categories for a double standard room are as follows:

$ = under 2,000 baht
$$ = 2,000–3,000 baht
$$$ = 3,000–5,000 baht
$$$$ = above 5,000 baht

Bangkok

The Conrad Bangkok
All Seasons Place
87 Witthayu (Wireless) Road
Tel: 0-2690 9999; Fax: 0-2690 9000
www.conradbangkok.com
This hotel with wireless access throughout the building for its business clientele. Excellent choice of chic restaurants and bars. $$$$

Four Seasons Hotel Bangkok
155 Ratchadamri Road
Tel: 0-2250 1000; Fax: 0-2253 9195
www.fourseasons.com/bangkok

Award-winning hotel with ideal location for shopping. Houses several sophisticated restaurants. Try a spa treatment in the minimalist Health Club designed by New York style guru Tony Chi. $$$$

The Metropolitan
27 South Sathorn Road
Tel: 0-2652 3333
This contemporary East-meets-West boutique hotel is situated in the business district and houses The Met, one of Bangkok's chicest lounge bars. Also has two popular restaurants: Cyan for Mediterranean food and Glow for organic dishes. $$$$

The Oriental Hotel
48 Oriental Avenue, New Road
Tel: 0-2659 9000; Fax: 0-2659 0000
www.mandarin-oriental.com/bangkok
Celebrated award-winning riverside hotel. Superb range of restaurants, including alfresco terrace dining. The Oriental Spa and Oriental Cookery School, both situated across the river in a colonial house, are highly respected institutions. Expect top class service. $$$$

Sheraton Grande Sukhumvit
250 Sukhumvit Road
Tel: 0-2649 8888; Fax: 0-2649 8000
www.sheratongrandesukhumvit.com
Luxury hotel right in the heart of Sukhumvit Road's shopping, restaurant and entertainment centres. Popular with both business and upmarket leisure travellers. $$$$

The Sukhothai Bangkok
13/3 South Sathorn Road
Tel: 0-2344 8888; Fax: 0-2344 8899
www.sukhothai.com
Quiet and private, with a boutique hotel feel.

Right: terrace, The Oriental hotel

Sophisticated, modern Thai decor. A clientele of mainly wealthy visitors and business travellers. Some of the best restaurants in town, including La Scala. $$$$

Ambassador
171 Sukhumvit Soi 11
Tel: 0-2254 0444; Fax: 0-2253 4123
www.amtel.co.th
A sprawling hotel that is only a 2-minute walk from Nana BTS. Wide range of restaurants on its premises. Popular with large tour groups. $$$

Baiyoke Sky Hotel
130 Rajaprop Road
Tel: 0-2656 3000; Fax: 0-2656 3555
www.baiyokehotel.com
At 88 storeys, the hotel is Bangkok's tallest, and on a clear day you can see forever. It is surrounded by countless garment shops and street vendors. $$$

The Bangkok Marriott Resort & Spa
257/1-3 Charoen Nakhorn Road, Thonburi
Tel: 0-2476 0022; Fax: 0-2476 1120
www.marriott.com
This lush riverside resort provides a perfect city escape, yet from their private ferry pier, it is still only minutes from BTS station. Self-contained, with six restaurants, three bars and a full-service business centre. The exceptional Mandara Spa is set in pretty gardens and has sumptuous Thai decor. $$$

Grand President
16 Sukhumvit Road, Soi 11
Tel: 0-2651 1200; Fax: 0-2651 1260
www.grandpresident.com
Great for families or business executives; 5-minute walk from the Nana BTS. All rooms have small kitchenettes. Three large pools and a gymnasium; buffet breakfast is included. $$$

Ayutthaya
U Thong Inn
210 Rojana Road
Tel: 0-3524 2236; Fax: 0-3524 2235
www.uthonginn.com
Offering mid-range accommodations with modern facilities, close to most of the attractions; popular with group tours. $

Kanchanaburi
Felix River Kwai
9/1 Moo 3, Tha Makham Village
Tel: 0-3451 5061; Fax: 0-3451 5095
www.felixriverkwai.co.th
Only 6km from the city, but close to Kanchanburi Bridge Station, this resort-style property has two pools by the riverfront. All deluxe rooms have water views. $–$$

Hua Hin
Evason Hua Hin Resort & Spa
9 Moo 3, Paknampran Beach, Pranburi
Tel: 0-3263 2111; Fax: 0-3263 2112
www.evasonresorts.com
Modern elegance along an isolated beach with the option of private pool villas. The Evason Spa offers a range of treatments in its minimalist but stylish environs. $$$$

Aleenta
183 Moo 4, Paknampran, Pranburi
Tel: 0-3257 0194; Fax: 0-3257 0220
www.aleenta.com
Small and intimate with only 10 villas. Rooms are spacious; most come with private plunge pools. Quiet location; about 30 minutes by car from Hua Hin. $$$

Anantara Resort & Spa
43/1 Phet Kasem Road
Tel: 0-3252 0250; Fax: 0-3252 0259
www.anantara.com
Well appointed and close to town on a pleasant stretch of sand. The resort caters to families as well as romantics, with its spacious lagoon rooms and its separate pool, plus the courtyard-style Mandara Spa. $$$

Sofitel Central Hua Hin Resort & Village
1 Damnoen Kasem
Tel: 0-3251 2021/38; Fax: 0-3251 1014
www.sofitel.com
The former Railway Hotel has kept its colonial charm and brought modern amenities to delightful historical surroundings. $$$

Hilton Hua Hin
33 Naresdamri Road
Tel: 0-3253 8999; Fax: 0-3253 8990
www.hilton.com
The Hilton has renovated this large hotel on the beach, 200m (220yd) from the main city

centre with good ocean frontage. Great views from the White Lotus Chinese Restaurant and a lively brewhouse-cum-disco. $$

Pattaya

Sheraton Pattaya
437 Pratamnak Road
Tel: 0-3825 9888; Fax: 0-3825 9899
www.sheraton.com/pattaya
The beautiful resort has calming water elements and its own beach. Many of the rooms have ocean-facing pavilions, and the Amburaya Spa is there for body tuning. $$$–$$$$

Amari Orchid Resort
Beach Road, North Pattaya
Tel: 0-3842 8161; Fax: 0-3842 8165
www.amari.com/orchid
This 230-room hotel, which is part of the Amari chain, is located on the quieter northern end of Pattaya beach. It has comfortable rooms, with views of either the beach or the gardens. $$–$$$

Chiang Mai

Four Seasons Resort Chiang Mai
Mae Rim-Samoeng Old Road, Mae Rim
Tel: 0-5329 8181; Fax: 0-5329 8190
www.fourseasons.com/chiangmai
Set among working rice paddies, the splendid scenery makes this deluxe resort's remote location even more attractive. The outstanding Lanna Spa offers traditional Thai treatments and a stunning hill-top Lanna Cookery School. $$$$

Tamarind Village
50/1 Ratchadamnoen Road
Tel: 0-5341 8898/9; Fax: 0-5341 8900
www.tamarindvillage.com
Classy boutique hotel with a smart, contemporary feel that is very popular. Delightful swimming pool and garden with mature trees and shrubs. A 15-minute walk to the night market. $$$

Amari Rincome
1 Nimmanhemin Road
Tel: 0-5322 1130; Fax: 0-5322 1915
www.amari.com/rincome
Situated on the edge of town, this old property is efficiently managed. Good restaurants and a superb swimming pool. $$

River View Lodge
25 Charoen Prathet Road
Tel: 0-5327 1109; Fax: 0-5327 9019
www.riverviewlodgch.com
Simple but spacious rooms in this riverside lodge set amid a pleasant garden, with tiny pool. Set right back from the busy road yet within walking distance of the shops and internet cafés. Great for breakfast. $

Sukhothai

Thai Village Hotel
214 Moo 3, Muangkao, Muang
Tel: 0-5569 7249; 0-5569 7583
www.thaivillagehotel.com
Beautiful teak building set in a large garden along the busy canal, with a good local restaurant. Rates include a buffet breakfast. $

Chiang Rai

Anantara Resort Golden Triangle
229 Moo 1, Chiang Saen
Tel: 0-5378 4084; Fax: 0-5378 4090
www.anantara.com
This 65-ha (160-acre) riverside property about 75km (47 miles) from Chiang Rai provides affordable luxury with superb views of the Golden Triangle area. Lush gardens, a first-class spa and a working elephant camp make the hour-long drive from the city to the resort very worthwhile. $$$

Dusit Island Resort
1129 Kraisora Sit Road
Tel: 0-5371 5777; Fax: 0-5371 5801
chiangrai.dusit.com
Located on an island a little way out of the main city, this modern hotel block takes pride of place in gardens overlooking the Kok River. There are river and garden view rooms, outdoor dining and a wide range of sports facilities. $$$

Mae Hong Son

Imperial Tara Mae Hong Son Hotel
149 Moo 8, Tambon Pang Moo
Tel: 0-5361 1021/25; Fax: 0-5361 1252
www.imperialhotels.com/taramaehongson
Though a little far from the city, this large resort built in the Northern-style provides the city's main upmarket accommodation. It has enormous gardens and is self-sufficient and close to trekking routes. $$

Nakhon Ratchasima (Khorat)

Royal Princess Hotel
1137 Sura Nari Road
Tel: 0-4425 6629; Fax: 0-4425 6601
korat.royalprincess.com
This comfortable property is designed in traditional Thai style. Restaurant has a good reputation for its Khorat and Chinese cuisine. Right in the the city centre. *$$*

Old Phimai Guest House
214 Moo 14, Chonsudaset Road, Phimai
Tel/Fax: 0-4447 1918
Suitable for those wanting to avoid the city and be close to the temple ruins. This simple hotel made of wood provides a restful atmosphere and a lovely roof garden.*$*

Ubon Ratchathani

Ubonburi Hotel Resort
1 Sri Mongkol Road, Warinchamrab District
Tel: 0-4526 6777; Fax: 0-4526 6770
www.ubonburihotel.com
About 25 minutes from the main downtown shopping district, this hotel with a swimming pool is popular with local business people. *$$*

Phuket

Amanpuri
118/1 Moo 3, Choeng Talay, Talang
Tel: 0-7632 4333; Fax: 0-7632 4100
www.amanresorts.com
This world-famous retreat is considered to be in a class of its own, well patronised by celebrities. Its 40 pavilions and 30 villas are on a steep hill leading down to a sun terrace and the celebrated dark-tile swimming pool. *$$$$*

JW Marriott Resort and Spa
231 Moo 3, Mai Khao, Talang
Tel: 0-7633 8000; Fax: 0-7634 8348
www.marriott.com
This delightful resort set among lagoons and ponds was carefully designed to minimise encroachment on the 17-km (10½-mile)-long beach where turtles come to lay eggs annually. Smart and casual dining, as well as a newly expanded Mandara Spa. *$$$$*

Le Royal Meridien Phuket Yacht Club
23/3 Viset Road, Nai Harn
Tel: 0-7638 0200; Fax: 0-7638 0280
www.yacht-club.phuket.com
Cleverly designed to hug a hill, it has easy access to a lovely white-sand beach at the southern end of Phuket. Rooms are expansive and tastefully furnished. *$$$$*

Mom Tri's Boathouse & Villa Royale
2/2 Patak Road, Kata Beach
Tel: 0-7633 0015; Fax: 0-7633 0561
www.boathousephuket.com
Small beachside hotel on Kata beach named after the Thai architect who designed it. In addition to its well-known beach restaurant, the hotel has built six luxurious private villas perched on the cliff and overlooking the adjacent Kata Noi bay. *$$$–$$$$*

Impiana Phuket Cabana
41 Thaweewong Road, Patong Beach
Tel: 0-7634 0138; Fax: 0-7634 0178
www.impiana.com
Comfortable resort catering to families and couples right across from Patong beach, but

Above: Pavilion interior, Rayavadee Resort

shielded from the busy road noise by a pleasant garden. The night market, bars and shops are only a few minutes' walk away. *$$$*

Katathani Resort
14 Kata Noi Road, Kata Noi Beach
Tel: 0-7633 0124; Fax: 0-7633 0426
www.katathani.com
Located right on beautiful Kata Noi beach, this old but well-maintained resort opened a new wing in late 2003. *$$–$$$*

Central Karon Village
701 Patak Road, Karon Beach
Tel: 0-7628 6300; Fax 0-7639 6793
www.centralhotelsresorts.com
With villas built along delightful winding paths on 22-ha (54-acres) of lawns and beach, this small resort offers tranquillity and seclusion from the main beaches. *$$*

Krabi Town
Krabi Maritime Park & Spa Resort
1 Tungfah Road, Krabi Town
Tel: 0-7562 0028; Fax: 0-7561 9929
www.maritimeparkandspa.com
Good for staying overnight in town, this large resort-style low-rise is built around a lagoon with landscaped gardens. *$$*

Krabi Beaches
Rayavadee Resort
214 Moo 2, Ao Nang, Muang
Tel: 0-7562 0740/3; Fax: 0-7620 630
www.rayavadee.com
With two-storey pavilions set in coconut groves next to huge cliffs and bordering three beaches. Full range of amenities including restaurants, spa and sports facilities. *$$$$*

Railay Bay Resort & Spa
Railay West Beach
Tel: 0-7562 2570; Fax: 0-7562 2573
www.krabi-railaybay.com
Different styles of cottages here, all with cable TV and air conditioning. Restaurant and pool on site, plus the Sunset Bar for drinks and great sunset views on Railay West beach. *$$*

Ko Lanta
Pimalai Resort & Spa
99 Moo 5, Ba Kan Tiang Beach
Tel: 0-7560 7999; Fax: 0-7560 7998
www.pimalai.com
A contemporary and stylish resort, with rooms and villas set in landscaped gardens facing lovely Ba Kan Tiang beach. Smart and casual dining overlooking the infinity pool and at the beachside restaurant. Accessible from mainland Krabi by a combination of car and boat. *$$$$*

Phi Phi
Holiday Inn Resort
Laem Thong Beach, Ko Phi Phi Don
Tel: 0-7562 1334; Fax: 0-1476 3787
www.phiphi-palmbeach.com
Depending on the season, this smart resort goes from mid- to high-range in price. Its location at the remote northern end of the beautiful island means guests enjoy tranquillity. Sightseeing is best accomplished by boat. *$$–$$$*

Phi Phi Banyan Villa
Ton Sai Beach, Ko Phi Phi Don
Tel: 0-7561 1233
www.phiphi-hotel.com
Located in the centre of Ao Ton Sai. The beach, restaurants, shops and pier are just 5 minutes' walk away. Comfortable rooms have air conditioning, cable TV and hot water. *$–$$*

Ko Samui
Buri Rasa Village
11/2 Moo 2, Chaweng Beach
Tel: 0-7723 0222; Fax: 0-7723 1838
www.burirasa.com
This lovely boutique resort is tastefully designed with a Thai village ambience. Rooms feature four-poster beds, DVD players and Wi-Fi internet access. *$$$–$$$$*

Imperial Boat House
83 Moo 5, Choeng Mon Beach
Tel: 0-2261 9000; Fax: 0-2261 9518
www.imperialboathouse.com
The northern promontory location is one of the most peaceful. The teak barge accommodation and boat-shaped pool give this upmarket resort a unique nautical flavour. Excellent dining overlooking the bay. *$$$*

The Tamarind Retreat
205/7 Moo 4, Thong Takien
Tel: 0-7742 4221; Fax: 0-7742 4311
www.tamarindretreat.com
A stunning hillside location among coconut trees and granite boulders, some of which are incorporated into this residential and day spa's minimalist architecture. Each self-contained villa has individual features such as a koi pond and Japanese *shoji* windows. *$$$*

Laem Set Inn & Spa
110 Moo 2, Hua Thanon
Tel: 0-7723 3299; Fax: 0-7742 4394
www.laemset.com
Collection of Thai-style rooms, suites and beach bungalows set in landscaped gardens. Its restaurant is famed for its excellent cuisine and cooking courses. *$$–$$$*

HEALTH AND EMERGENCIES

Hygiene / General Health
Tap water is not safe. Drink bottled water or soft drinks and use tap water only for bathing and brushing teeth.

Stomach upsets are normally caused by over-indulgence. Many foreigners overeat and their stomachs react negatively to a sudden switch of food. Two rules: don't eat the skin of any fresh fruit; don't eat sweets from street carts as the desserts are not fresh.

Sunburn is a problem; patients have been admitted with first and second degree burns, so apply sun block lotion generously.

Malaria has been reduced in the North, but it is still a problem, usually in villages. Dengue fever is common on the islands. If trekking, sleep under a mosquito net and apply mosquito repellent. Maloprim and other prophylactics are virtually useless.

Medical / Dental Services
First-class hotels have doctors on call to treat medical emergencies. For more serious cases, the ambulance service and hospitals are comparable to that in major Western cities, with Intensive Care Units equipped to handle most emergencies.

These days Thailand is positioning itself as a centre for inexpensive medical treatments and surgery. Increasingly, people fit in a full medical examination while on holiday in Bangkok.

Bangkok: Bumrungrad International (tel: 0-2667 1000; www.bumrungrad.com), 33 Sukhumvit Soi 3 (Nana BTS).
Chiang Mai: McCormick Hospital (tel: 0-5326 2200), Kaew Nawarat Road.
Phuket: Phuket International Hospital (tel: 0-7624 9400; www.phuket-inter-hospital. co.th), 44 Chalermprakiat Ror 9 Road.

Pharmacies
Pharmaceuticals are produced to international standards, and most pharmacies have registered pharmacists (with a pharmaceutical reference book) on the premises. Pharmacy personnel in the many branches of the Boots chain speak English.

Crime
Thailand is generally free of violent crime towards foreigners but be wary nonetheless. With increased tourist arrivals, pickpockets are on the rise. Beware of those offering free tours or directing you to shops offering special prices. Avoid all offers of free drinks, even on public buses where hostesses serve refreshments. Crime against tourists is fairly rare, but there have been reported cases of knock-out drugs slipped into drinks by 'friendly' bar staff at some of the city's sleazier nightspots.

Police
Bangkok: The police emergency number is 191. There is also a Tourist Police Unit (tel: 1155) formed specially to assist travellers. Find them at the Tourist Assistance Centre at the Tourism Authority of Thailand (TAT) headquarters, and on the corner of Rama 4 and Silom roads.
Chiang Mai: Tourist Police, tel: 0-5324 8974.
Phuket: Tourist Police, tel: 0-7622 5361.

COMMUNICATIONS AND NEWS

Post

Post offices are open Monday to Friday 8.30am–4.30pm and later depending on location. Most offer postal services, overseas phone calls and courier services.

Telephone

Thailand's telephone system is modern and efficient. Local and international calls can be made from hotels, phone booths and from general post offices in provincial capitals. Most hotels also have mail, e-mail and fax facilities. First-class hotel rooms have IDD phones; others have operators. To call abroad, dial the international access code 001, followed by the country code.

Since 2002, area codes (including the prefix zero) must always be dialled when making local calls within the same city and when calling from one province to another. If calling from overseas, drop the prefix zero.

The country code for Thailand is 66. Area codes for the places of interest covered in this guide are as follows: Bangkok: 02; Ayutthaya: 035; Kanchanaburi: 034; Hua Hin: 032; Pattaya: 038; Chiang Mai, Chiang Rai and Mae Hong Son: 053; Sukhothai: 055; Nakhon Ratchasima (Khorat): 044; Ubon Ratchathani: 045; Phuket: 076; Krabi and Phi Phi: 075; Ko Samui: 077.

For directory assistance in Bangkok dial 1133; for operator assistance with domestic calls dial 101; for international calls dial 100. Note that any telephone number beginning with 08 indicates a cellular telephone, and the zero must be dialled.

Only users of GSM 900 OR GSM 1800 mobile phones with international roaming facility can hook up automatically to the local Thai network. Check with your service provider if you're not sure.

Media

The *Bangkok Post* and *The Nation* are among the best and most com-prehensive English-language dailies. The *Asian Wall Street Journal* and the *International Herald Tribune* and editions of British, French and German newspapers are available at major hotels, or at good bookstores. Try **BK Magazine** for up-to-date listings of things to do and where to go in Bangkok.

USEFUL INFORMATION

Export Permits for Antiques

The Fine Arts Department (tel: 0-2226 1661) prohibits the export of all Buddha images, images of other deities, and fragments (hands or heads) of images created before the 18th century. Shops can register other art objects for you, or you can take the items and two postcard-sized photographs of each item to the Fine Arts Department on Na Prathat Road in Bangkok.

USEFUL ADDRESSES

Tourist Information

Tourism Authority of Thailand (TAT)
The head office of the **Bangkok** Tourism Authority of Thailand is at 1600 New Phetchaburi Road, Makkason, Rachathewi, tel: 0-2250 5500; fax: 0-2250 5511.
TAT Call Centre: 1672 (8am–8pm).
Alternatively, visit TAT's branch office at 4 Ratchadamnoen Nok or at Suvarnabhumi Airport's Arrival Hall.
Chiang Mai TAT (tel: 0-5324 8604) is at 105/1 Chiang Mai-Lamphun Road.
Phuket TAT (tel: 0-7621 1036) is at 73–75 Phuket Road, Phuket Town.

Useful Websites

Tourism Authority of Thailand
www.tourismthailand.org
Bangkok Tourist Bureau
www.bangkoktourist.com
Bangkok Post
www.bangkokpost.com
Bangkok Metro Magazine
www.bkkmetro.com
Association of Thai Travel Agents
www.atta.or.th
Hotel Booking Service
www.thailandhotels.com

Right: postal drop

ACKNOWLEDGEMENTS

Cover	**Walter Bibikow**
Backcover Top	**Luca Invernizzi Tettoni/Photobank**
Backcover Bottom	**Josef Beck**
Photography	**Marcus Wilson Smith/APA and**
Pages 79	**Courtesy of Oriental Hotel**
74B	**D. Saulnier/HBL**
73	**Josef Beck**
88	**David Bowden**
74T, 85	**Matthew Burns/Asia Images**
93	**Joe Cummings/CPA**
1	**Alain Evrard**
83	**Marcus Gortz**
71	**Oliver Hargreave/CPA**
2/3, 8/9, 20, 31, 61B, 63, 68	**David Henley/CPA**
12	**Hans Höfer**
10, 11, 13T, 43T, 43B, 59, 64, 65, 69, 86, 87	**Luca Invernizzi Tettoni**
23, 33, 35B, 77	**Ingo Jezierski**
72, 90	**Rainer Krack/CPA**
78	**Jason Lang/APA**
36, 37	**Derrick Lim/APA**
97	**JW Marriott Resort and Spa**
98	**Leonardo Media**
7T, 13B, 14, 15, 24, 25B, 42, 49, 52B,	
55T, 57, 61T, 70, 81, 82, 89, 96	**Steve Van Beek**
30	**Rachot Visalarnkul**
76	**VPA Images**
Cartography	**Maria Donnelly**
Cover Design	**Carlotta Junger**
Production	**Caroline Low**

INDEX